CW01666474

COVER BIRDS

Robert Gillmor, as this book describes, started his long career as an illustrator at the age of thirteen with his first design for the recently formed Reading Ornithological Club. By the age of fifteen he was drawing for the distinguished monthly magazine, *British Birds*. He illustrated the first of over one hundred books in 1958, while an art student at Reading University. In the late fifties, with the support of leading bird artists of the day, he organised *Exhibition by Contemporary Bird Painters*, and this led directly to the founding in 1964 of the Society of Wildlife Artists, of which he is currently vice-president. He is a keen ornithologist and has served on council for the RSPB, the British Ornithologists' Union and the British Trust for Ornithology.

His masterful linocuts have graced book jackets, greetings cards, posters and stamps, the latter being the subject of his first Two Rivers Press book, *Birds, Blocks and Stamps*, 2012. His work perfectly captures the essence of his subjects – what ornithologists call 'the jizz'.

BY THE SAME AUTHOR

Joint author with Martin Davies & Tim Appleton. *The Art of Conservation. 25 Years of Birdfair Posters* (Red Hare Publishing, 2013)
Birds, Blocks & Stamps: Post & Go Birds of Britain (Two Rivers Press, 2012)
Joint author with Peter Marren. *Art of the New Naturalists* (Collins, 2009)
Cutting Away: the linocuts of Robert Gillmor (Langford Press, 2006)
What to see in our Nature Reserves. Activity Guide for Pupils (Encyclopaedia Britannica Ltd, 1966)

ALSO PUBLISHED BY TWO RIVERS PRESS

All Change at Reading: The railway and the station 1840–2013 by Adam Sowan
An Artist's Year in the Harris Garden by Jenny Halstead
Caversham Court Gardens: A Heritage Guide by Friends of Caversham Court Gardens
Believing in Reading: Our Places of Worship by Adam Sowan
Newtown: A Photographic Journey in Reading 1974 by Terry Allsop
Bikes, Balls & Biscuitmen: Our Sporting Life by Tim Crooks & Reading Museum
The Reading Quiz Book by Adam Sowan
Bizarre Berkshire: An A–Z Guide by Duncan Mackay
Reading Poetry: An Anthology edited by Peter Robinson
Reading: A Horse-Racing Town by Nigel Sutcliffe
Eat Wild by Duncan MacKay
Down by the River: The Thames and Kennet in Reading by Gillian Clark
A Much-maligned Town: Opinions of Reading 1126–2008 by Adam Sowan
A Mark of Affection by Adam Sowan
The Stranger in Reading edited by Adam Sowan
The Holy Brook by Adam Sowan
Charms against Jackals edited by Adam Stout and Geoff Sawers
Abattoirs Road to Zinzan Street by Adam Sowan

ROBERT GILLMOR

COVER BIRDS

TWO
RIVERS
PRESS

First published in the UK in 2013 by

Two Rivers Press
7 Denmark Road
Reading RG1 5PA
www.tworiverspress.com

ISBN 978-1-901677-96-6

1 2 3 4 5 6 7 8 9

Two Rivers Press is represented in the UK by Inpress Ltd
and distributed by Central Books

Cover illustration by Robert Gillmor
Text and cover design by Nadja Guggi

Typeset in Parisine
Printed and bound in Great Britain by Ashford Colour Press, Gosport

Foreword

The Berkshire (formerly Reading) Ornithological Club has had a long and fruitful connection with Robert Gillmor. Robert has the distinction of being the club's first junior member, having been extended a special invitation to attend the club's meetings notwithstanding his 'extreme youth' by the club's committee during the first year of its existence.

Robert served the club in various capacities over the subsequent years, as secretary, chairman and eventually president between 1971 and 1997, before he moved to Norfolk. During this period, Robert and Sue kindly hosted the club's committee meetings in their front room at Northcourt Avenue, providing refreshments to assist the sometimes protracted discussions.

Robert though has also contributed generously to the club's output in another way. He has produced the artwork for the cover of the club's annual bird report ever since the third one, for the year 1949.

It is typical of Robert's generosity that he has continued to provide these illustrations for us, notwithstanding the demands of being an artist and illustrator who is always in demand, with a long order book of commercial work. These covers are the subject of this book, which also provides some of the background behind the reports, the club and the birds that Robert illustrated. We are pleased to share Robert's work for us with you, and hope you will enjoy them too. You will appreciate the great debt of gratitude we owe him for this special contribution to the club.

Neil Bucknell
President, BOC

Acknowledgements

It is often the case with acknowledgements that wives and family come last, when in many cases they should be the very first to receive recognition of the part played in backing the writer. To Sue I owe my warmest thanks for her love and support. A book like this would never have happened without such sympathetic understanding.

It is a real delight for an author to work with such an efficient team as that at Two Rivers Press, so ably led by Sally Mortimore. Sorting out and placing such a disparate collection of illustrations fell to Nadja Guggi and I am more than pleased and grateful for the way she has solved the problem. Barbara Morris managed to turn pages of handwriting into readable text and encouraged me to expand or explain details that seemed brief or vague. To eleven-year-old Anna Hodgson I am very grateful for succinctly shortening my original six word title to two.

The Berkshire Ornithological Club is fortunate to be able to call on such a distinguished ornithologist as Neil Bucknell to lead it as President, and I am greatly appreciative of his most generous foreword. For over sixty years I have had the privilege of working with a succession of the Club's Recorders and Officers who have all been helpful and encouraging. I am sure that they did not realise how significant a part they have played in my career.

For Isabelle

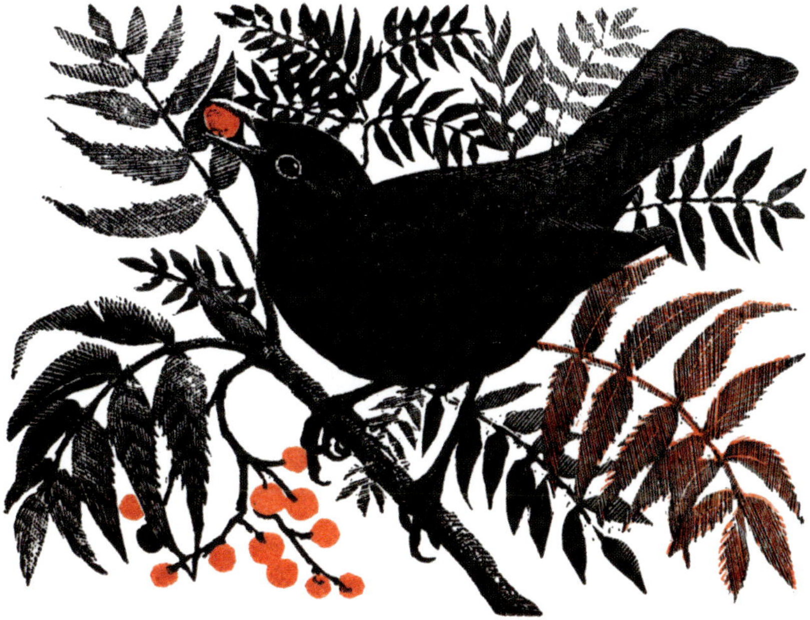

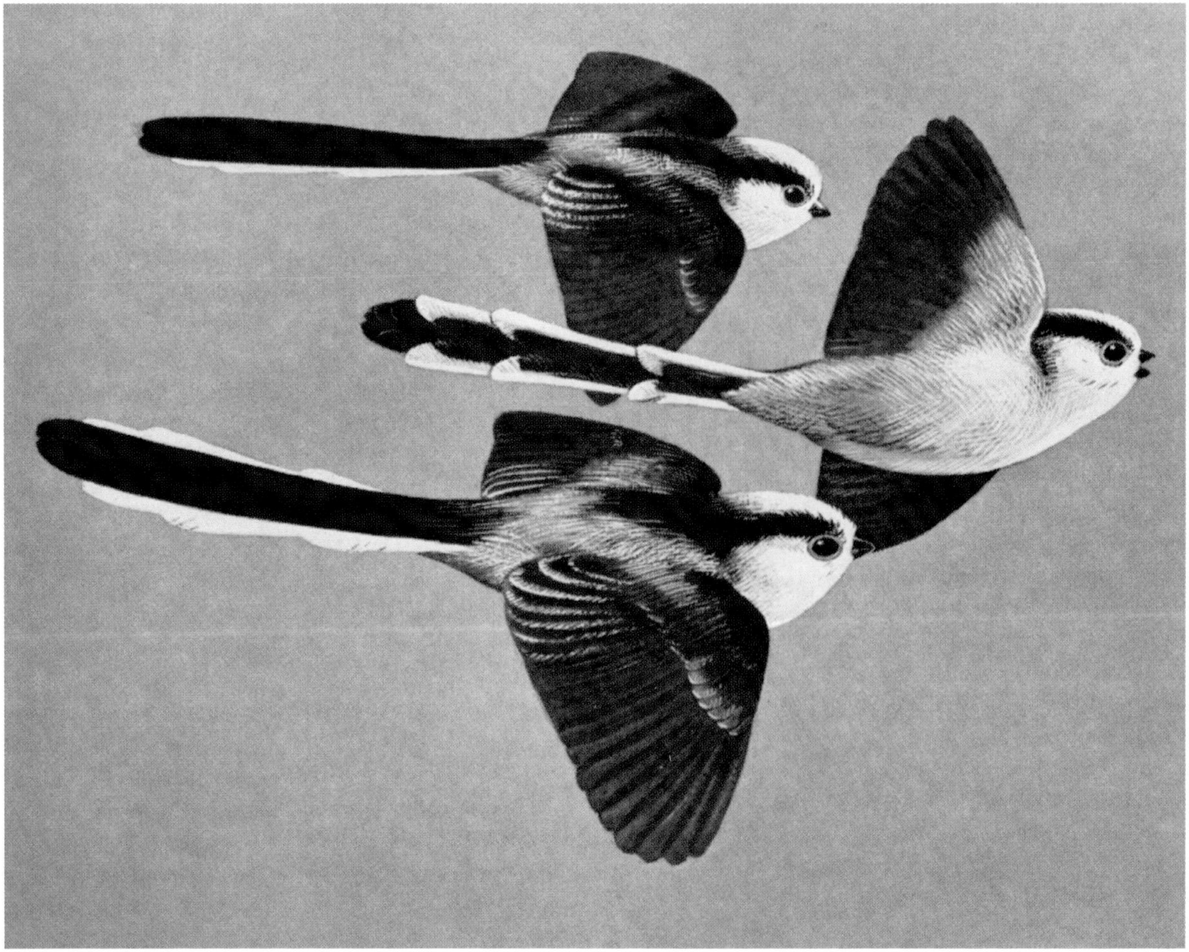

COVER BIRDS

It is fantastically encouraging for a young artist to see his or her work in print for the first time. I was extremely fortunate to have this experience at a very early age and am hugely grateful to those who encouraged me, even though that early work did not show as much promise as enthusiasm! In many ways I was lucky to be in the right place at the right time. The officers of the newly formed Reading Ornithological Club were certainly encouraging, allowing me to illustrate their precious early publications.

Local Bird Clubs still give such opportunities to budding artists. Annual Reports benefit from illustrations and many of today's most distinguished artists saw, like me, their youthful attempts cheering the pages of text which, at times, cried out for such cheer!

The Reading Ornithological Club (ROC) had been launched in the spring of 1947. Its founders, largely from the University, arrived at its name by combining the titles of the two leading University bird groups, the Oxford Ornithological Society and the Cambridge Bird Club. Early meetings were held in University science lecture theatres and the association with academia has continued to this day, some sixty-six years later. But it is not a University club, being rather more town than gown.

My involvement with the ROC started very soon after its formation. My enthusiasm for birds, already obvious at junior school, had led to my being taken to some of the meetings, the late evenings probably being an added attraction! I was far too young to be elected to membership, but in the minutes of a committee meeting held on 8 January 1948 it was resolved that 'Mr Gillmor on account of his extreme youth be encouraged to come along as a visitor.' I was, and particularly remember a lecture by James Fisher in March that year at the end of which I asked the great man to autograph my paperback of *Watching Birds.* James was at the forefront of post-war enthusiasm for natural history, and through his many broadcasts, articles and books, was the Attenborough of his day. He was one of the originators, and editors, of Collins' iconic *New Naturalist* series, first published in 1945, which sold in thousands to a nation exhausted by war and starved of contact with the natural world. The series is still going as strongly as ever, and now totals 125 volumes. I have been privileged to design their jackets since 1985. Some sixteen years after that memorable evening James opened the inaugural exhibition of the Society of Wildlife Artists which celebrates its 50th anniversary in 2013. Eventually, at the ripe old age of thirteen I was elected as the Club's first Junior Member, and within ten years I had taken on the office of Honorary Secretary.

I was more than fortunate, in all sorts of ways, that the distinguished ornithologist, J. Duncan Wood, was a master at Leighton Park, the Quaker school which I joined from the Junior School in 1949. He had been one of the founders of the ROC and acted as its first chairman. Formerly a pupil at the school, he had returned to the staff after service with the Friends Ambulance Unit in China. He ran the Bird Group which met every Friday evening during 'Hobby Hour'. This was one of the strongest of the many hobbies encouraged as a vital part of the school's ethos, and many of its members went on to play important roles in British ornithology. Duncan had been with parties to Skokholm Island, off Pembrokeshire, where they helped Ronald Lockley set up his bird observatory and build the first Heligoland and other traps. The Heligoland was a very large trap with a wide and high open mouth, planted with bird-attractive shrubs. Birds would be gently driven into the mouth which gradually narrowed to a catching box where the birds were gathered for ringing and, where appropriate, weighing and measuring. The trap was named after the first of its kind which had been

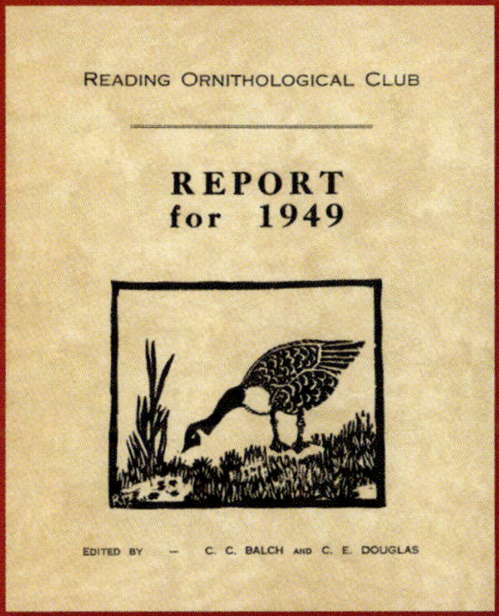
READING ORNITHOLOGICAL CLUB
REPORT
for 1949
EDITED BY — C. C. BALCH AND C. E. DOUGLAS

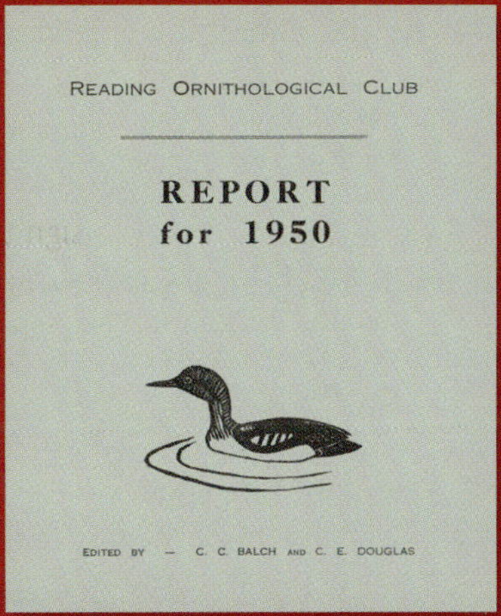
READING ORNITHOLOGICAL CLUB
REPORT
for 1950
EDITED BY — C. C. BALCH AND C. E. DOUGLAS

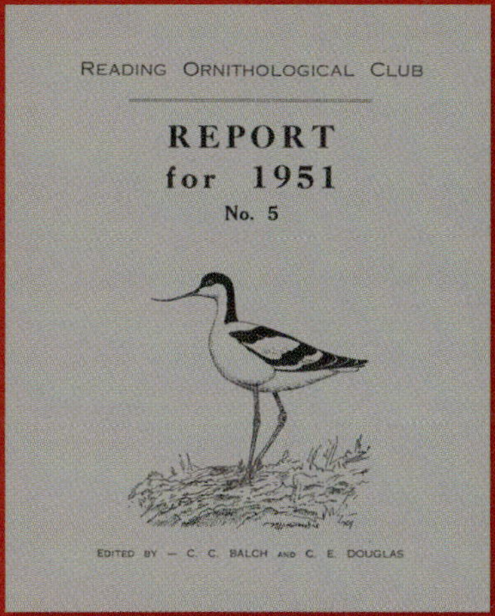
READING ORNITHOLOGICAL CLUB
REPORT
for 1951
No. 5
EDITED BY — C. C. BALCH AND C. E. DOUGLAS

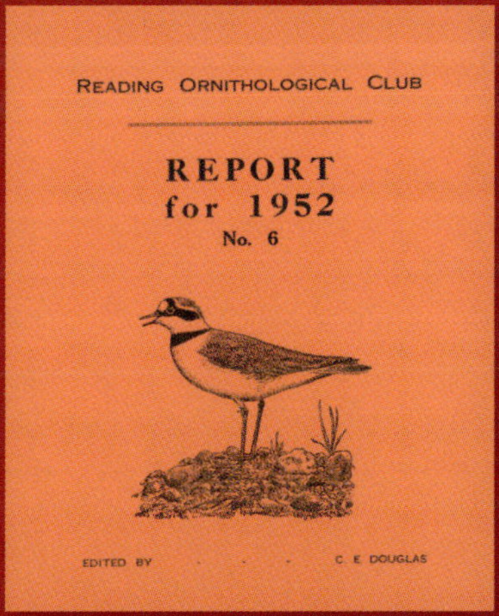
READING ORNITHOLOGICAL CLUB
REPORT
for 1952
No. 6
EDITED BY - - - C. E. DOUGLAS

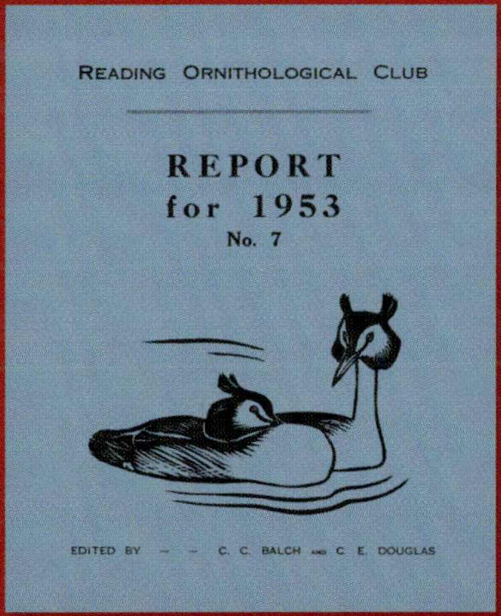
READING ORNITHOLOGICAL CLUB
REPORT
for 1953
No. 7
EDITED BY — — C. C. BALCH AND C. E. DOUGLAS

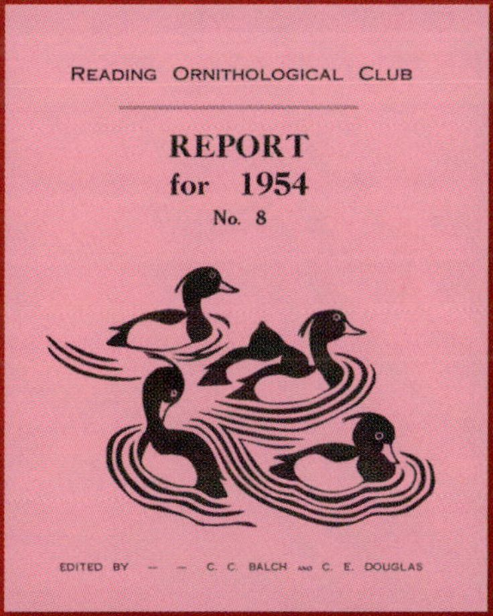
READING ORNITHOLOGICAL CLUB
REPORT
for 1954
No. 8
EDITED BY — — C. C. BALCH AND C. E. DOUGLAS

ROC Report for 1949. Canada Goose, linocut

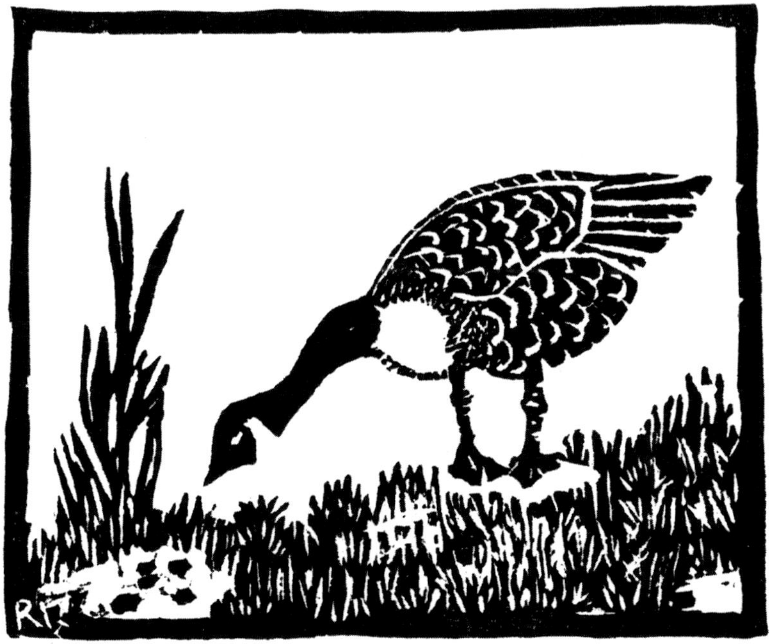

constructed on the German island of Heligoland, where one of the first bird observatories had been set up in 1909. Ronald had gone to live on the remote Welsh island as a young man and over thirteen years made detailed studies of several seabirds, one result being his classic book on the Manx Shearwater. At that time bird ringers could take their rings with them. Leighton Park School's ringing totals were headed by such expected species as Blue Tit and Blackbird, but high on the list was the essentially maritime Manx Shearwater, hardly a bird to be found nesting in Berkshire.

The Bird Group was run on formal lines, with a Chairman and a Secretary who kept minutes of each meeting – to be read, approved and signed at the following. We introduced and thanked visiting speakers and were indeed lucky to have several who could, and did, grace more erudite societies. All this led to a wonderful training, hugely benefitting those of us who were to go on into the world of organisations, committees and lecturing.

It was through Duncan that my illustration came to be used on the first printed cover of the ROC Annual Report, the subsequent designs being the main focus of this book. Our art master and fine craftsman, Harry Stevens, introduced us to lino cutting, and a small square print of a Canada Goose found its way on to the cover of the ROC's third report covering observations in 1949.

My school friend Nick Blurton Jones's great interest was in wildfowl and he had joined the Severn Wildfowl Trust in its first year, and I followed in the second. Canada Geese were not the ubiquitous bird we know today, but there was a small colony living in the private park surrounding Englefield House to the west of Reading between Theale and Bradfield. The geese were nesting on several islands in the park's Cranemoor Lake. We had permission to go there to study the colony and catch the birds for ringing in late summer when, during the moult, the adults are flightless. We rounded them up into a pen made from cricket and tennis nets borrowed from school. Here they were ringed, weighed and, in one year, had their backsides dyed bright blue with dye provided by the Wildfowl Trust. This made it a lot easier to follow their local movements as they spread out, away from the confines of the park. At this time, in the early fifties, a string of gravel pits was being developed along the Kennet Valley and these became important sites for the geese and many other species, such as the Great Crested Grebe and Little Ringed Plover, two birds I was to become involved with later.

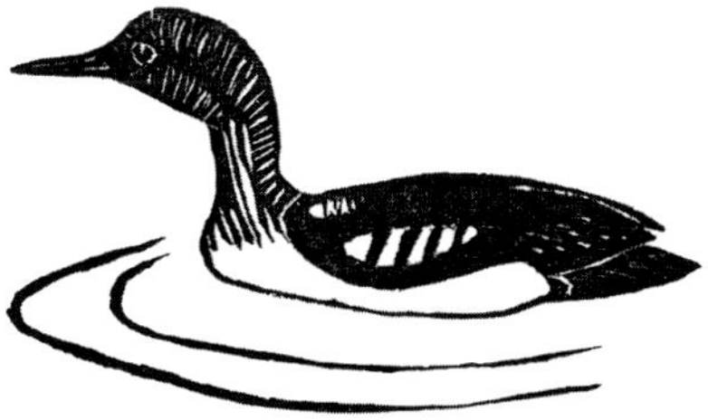

ROC Report for 1950. Black-Throated Diver, linocut

Incredibly, the Canada Goose linocut was not my first and last cover, but perhaps with no-one else to ask, I was given the chance to do the next. This was another linocut, and of a real rarity, a Black-throated

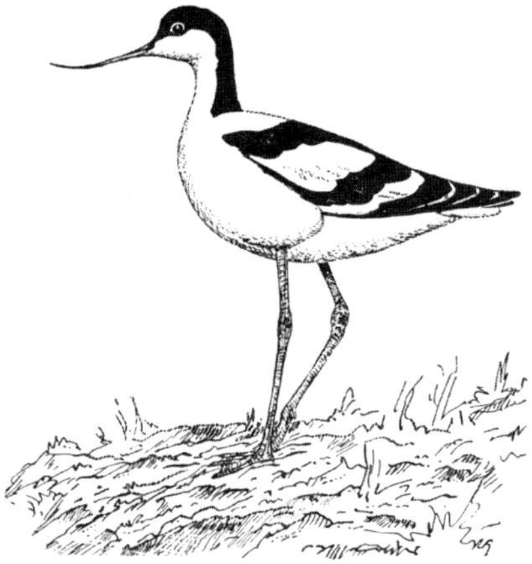

ROC Report for 1951. Avocet, scraperboard

Diver, which appeared on Whiteknights Park Lake, now on the campus of Reading University, on 3 February 1950 and stayed until 4 April. I remember watching it at close range from the road bordering the Lake, a glorious bird in full spring plumage. It should have been heading north, perhaps to join the small population on the larger lochs in north-west Scotland and the Outer Hebrides. Or perhaps further to Iceland where I would be watching them four years later. The same little block was also used on the cover of a *Provisional List of the Birds of Reading,* published in 1951.

The covers were printed at a small printing works at Sindlesham. The insides were duplicated on a Gestetner machine from typewritten sheets and stapled into the folded cover of thin, coloured card, a different colour each year. This method of production lasted for twenty-five years until 1973 when the whole Report was printed and reduced from quarto to the usual size (A5) for such publications.

The next two covers carried line drawings on scraperboard, each of 'special' birds. The Avocet had been found at Burghfield Gravel Pit by C.E. Douglas, one of the club's recorders, at 7 pm on 4 May, and several members managed to see it before dusk. Unfortunately it had moved on before others rushed to see it next morning. Avocets had recolonised England only a decade earlier, in the 1940s, and were still rare and exciting sightings. It was not until the mid-70s that they started to expand their range from Suffolk and gradually spread around the coast of East Anglia and to winter widely, especially in the south west.

I was certainly more familiar with the next bird on the 1952 report, the Little Ringed Plover. This attractive wader arrived in the area in 1949, eleven years after the first recorded nesting at Tring, and found an ideal habitat in the wide stretches of gravel around the flooded excavations of the new gravel workings, such as those at Burghfield. The reports of this period do not specify precise localities as the LRP, as we

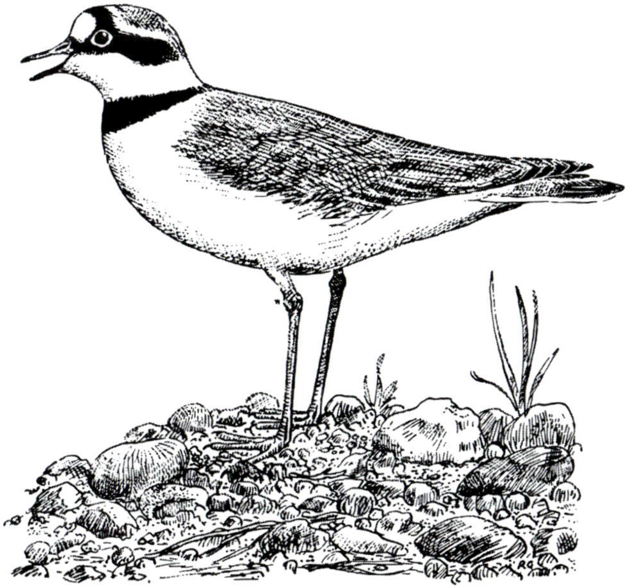

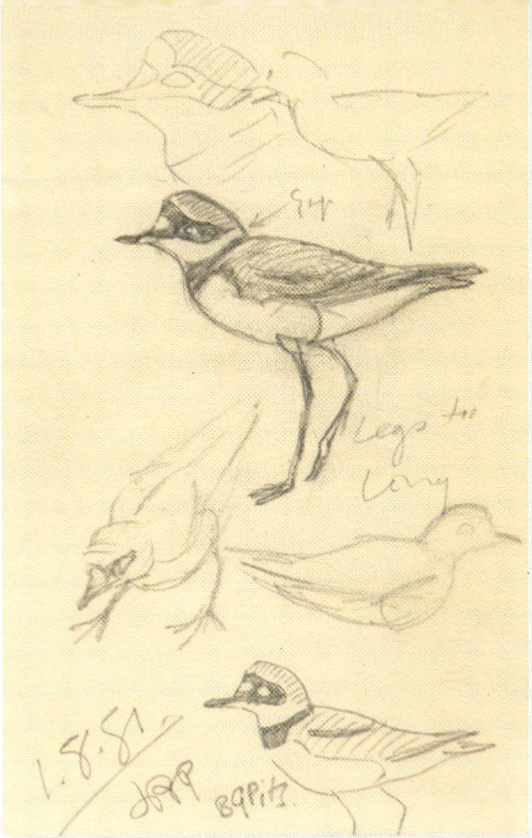

ROC Report for 1952. Little Ringed Plover, scraperboard

Field sketches for 1952 report. Little Ringed Plover

all knew the bird, was still an exciting, rare and somewhat exotic arrival. It is now widely distributed around England, particularly the south-east and Midlands where it can find suitable man-made habitats, like the Kennet Valley gravel pits.

The plovers attracted the attention of Ken Simmons, recently returned from National Service to take up a teaching post in Reading. He went on to make an extensive study of the life and behaviour of this charming plover. From 1962–1964 he went as schoolmaster to Ascension Island in the South Atlantic where he studied the breeding biology of the Brown Booby. This work gained him his MSc from Bristol University in 1967. He had become a professional ornithologist on his

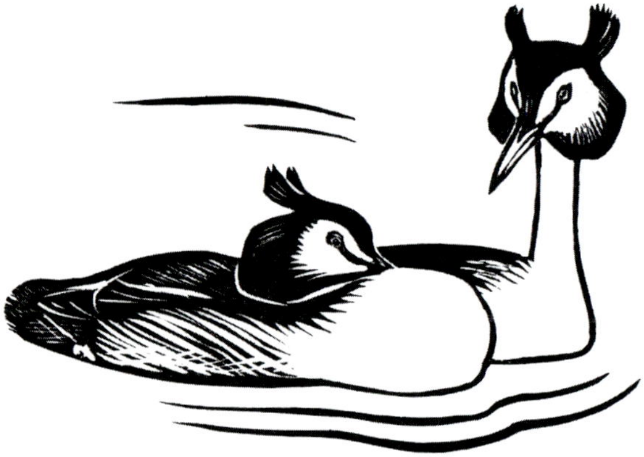

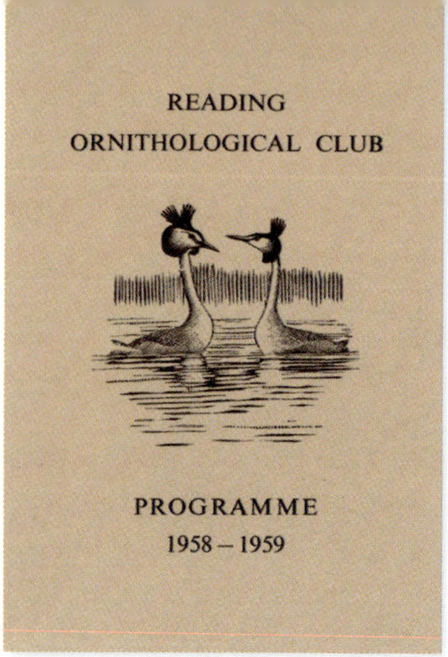

ROC Report for 1953. Great Crested Grebes, linocut

ROC Programme Card 1958–1959, wood engraving

return from Ascension and went on to receive a PhD from Bristol in 1970 for his work on the Great Crested Grebe. We were together on the editorial board of the *Birds of the Western Palearctic,* 1977–1994. Ken became a good friend and gave me the chance to illustrate his papers on LRP behaviour, leading me to watch and sketch the birds with great enthusiasm. The drawing is perhaps a bit stiff but it shows the difference in character between the LRP and the more familiar Ringed Plover. It is a more athletic-looking bird, slimmer with more restrained black head and chest markings. Although I had not seen a wild Avocet, I sketched them in the London Zoo wader aviaries in September 1952. Mine is not too bad, but the black areas of its wings look as if painted onto a smooth, white egg-shaped model.

For the 1953 report, I had again made a linocut, this time of Great Crested Grebes, and the cutting is much more assured and confident. This was another of Ken Simmons's study birds, which meant that I also was watching and sketching them with particular interest. Later I illustrated a series of papers Ken wrote for the *Avicultural Magazine*, which were published in 1953 and reprinted as a separate volume. The same

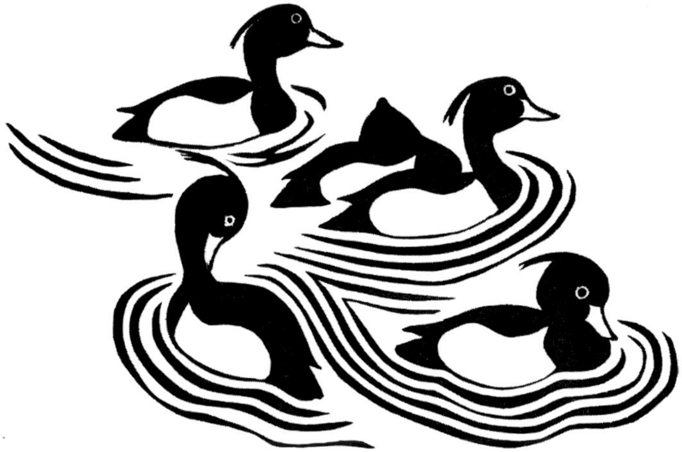

ROC Report for 1954. Tufted Ducks, linocut

report also contained an article by Nick and myself on ‘Catching Canada Geese’. It describes the catching and marking of 40 adults and goslings at Cranemoor Lake. The account has a regard for the proper order of things: ‘Shortly after 10.30 am work had started on the construction of a cage from cricket and tennis nets, and the collapsible boat was pinned together. When all preparations were completed, a picnic lunch was eaten and the team moved into action.’

The 1954 cover has the first appearance of the Tufted Duck, the bird eventually chosen for the Club’s logo. Its neat shape and bold black and white plumage make it an ideal subject, with no fussy detail to make reduction at a small size tricky. The linocut shows all drakes, whereas the duller brown females, lacking the tuft, are not so graphic. The design is also more ‘designerly’ than before, perhaps reflecting the changing, or developing, approach of the eighteen-year-old artist! The Tufted Duck is a widespread resident throughout Britain, the commonest of the diving ducks. It is another species that has exploited gravel workings, especially mature areas with more vegetation-rich borders, providing cover for nesting.

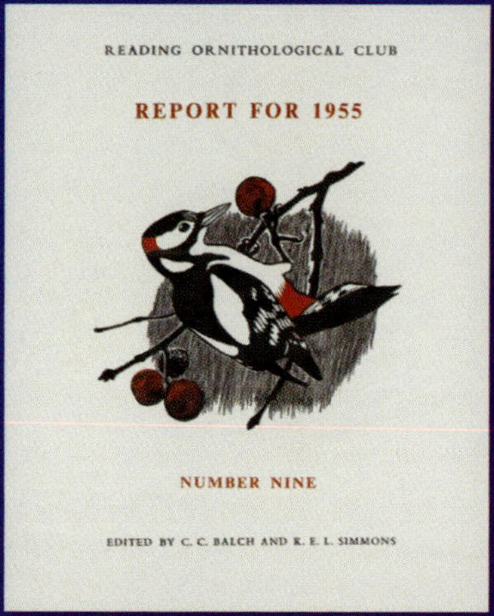
READING ORNITHOLOGICAL CLUB
REPORT FOR 1955
NUMBER NINE
EDITED BY C. C. BALCH AND K. E. L. SIMMONS

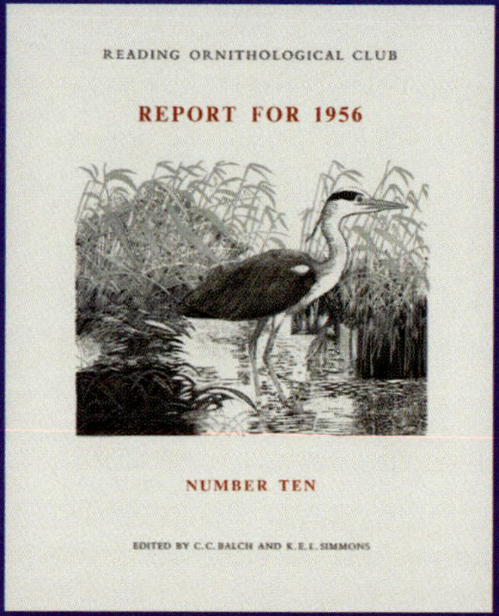
READING ORNITHOLOGICAL CLUB
REPORT FOR 1956
NUMBER TEN
EDITED BY C. C. BALCH AND K. E. L. SIMMONS

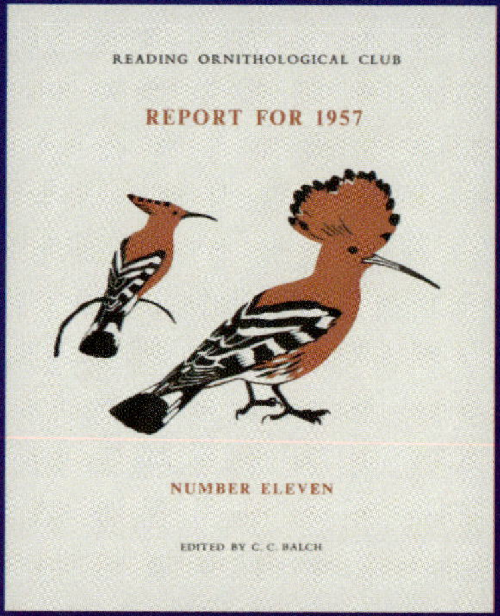
READING ORNITHOLOGICAL CLUB
REPORT FOR 1957
NUMBER ELEVEN
EDITED BY C. C. BALCH

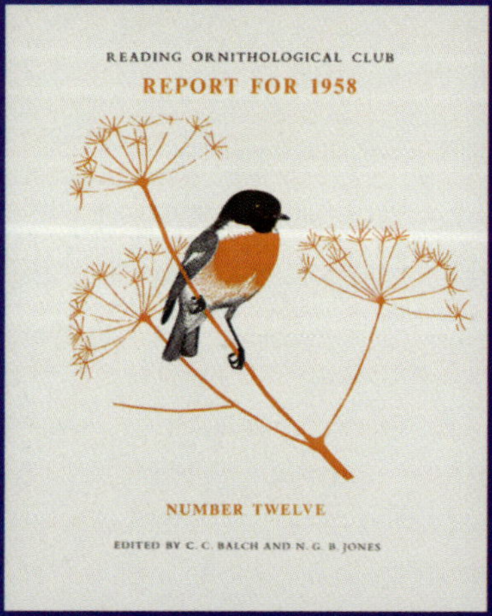
READING ORNITHOLOGICAL CLUB
REPORT FOR 1958
NUMBER TWELVE
EDITED BY C. C. BALCH AND N. G. B. JONES

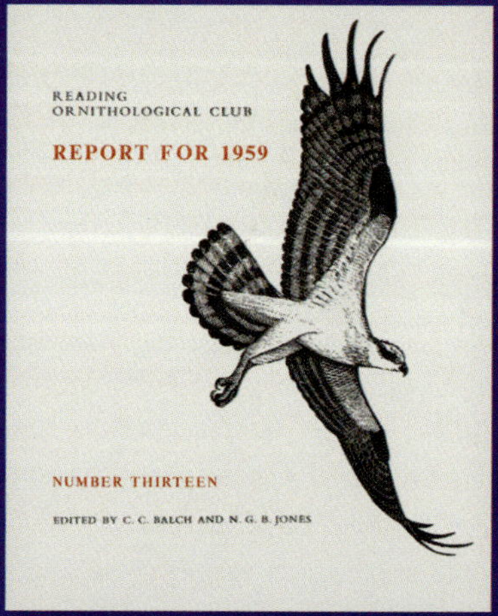
READING
ORNITHOLOGICAL CLUB
REPORT FOR 1959
NUMBER THIRTEEN
EDITED BY C. C. BALCH AND N. G. B. JONES

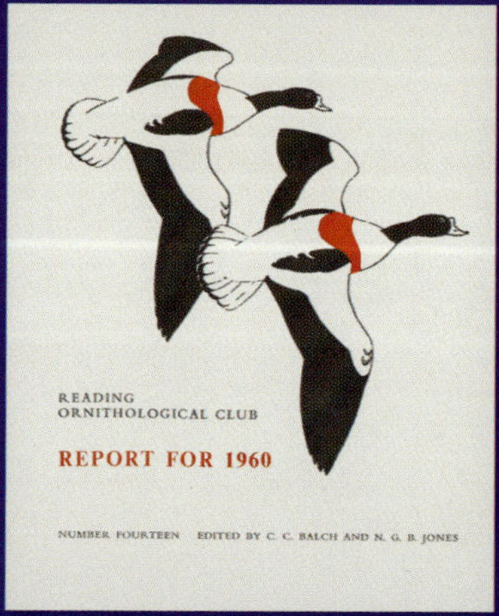
READING
ORNITHOLOGICAL CLUB
REPORT FOR 1960
NUMBER FOURTEEN
EDITED BY C. C. BALCH AND N. G. B. JONES

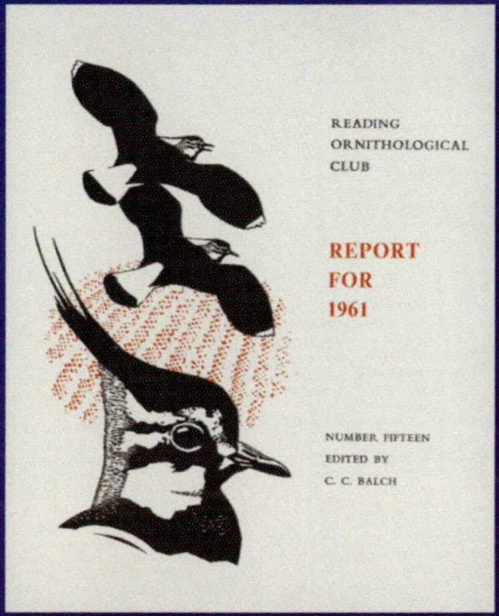
READING ORNITHOLOGICAL CLUB
REPORT FOR 1961
NUMBER FIFTEEN
EDITED BY
C. C. BALCH

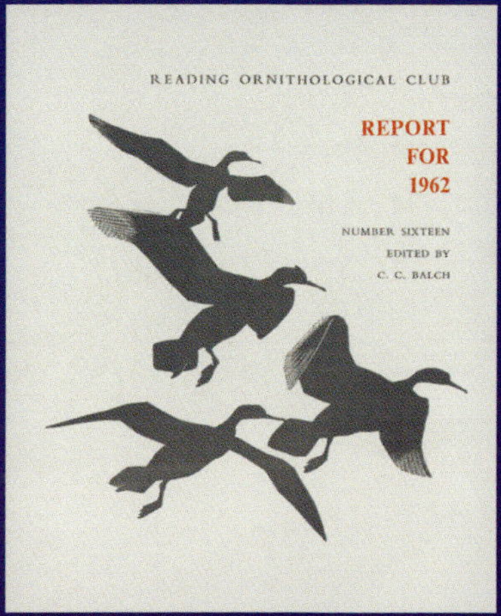
READING ORNITHOLOGICAL CLUB
REPORT FOR 1962
NUMBER SIXTEEN
EDITED BY
C. C. BALCH

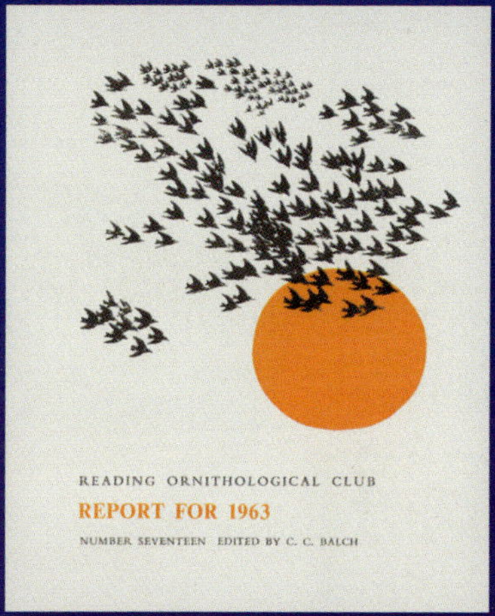
READING ORNITHOLOGICAL CLUB
REPORT FOR 1963
NUMBER SEVENTEEN EDITED BY C. C. BALCH

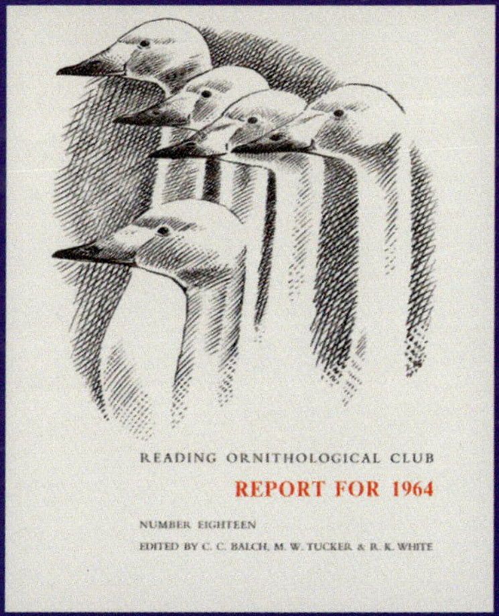
READING ORNITHOLOGICAL CLUB
REPORT FOR 1964
NUMBER EIGHTEEN
EDITED BY C. C. BALCH, M. W. TUCKER & R. K. WHITE

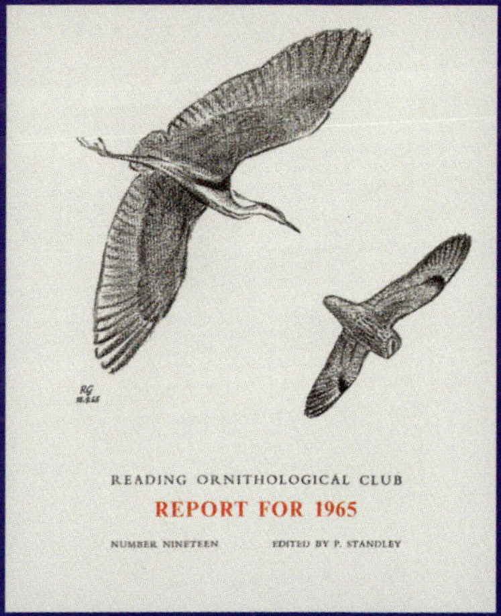
READING ORNITHOLOGICAL CLUB
REPORT FOR 1965
NUMBER NINETEEN
EDITED BY P. STANDLEY

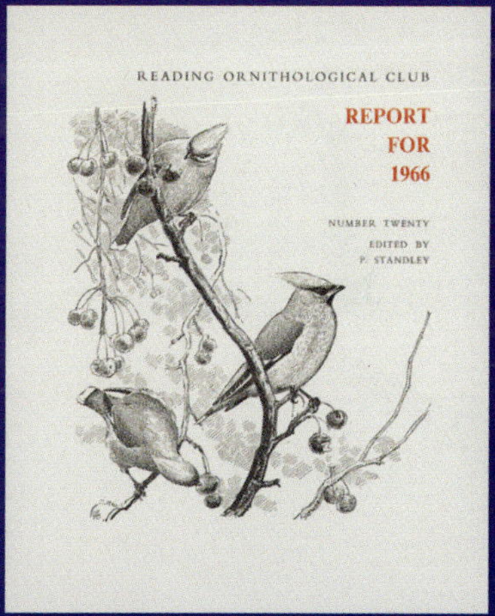
READING ORNITHOLOGICAL CLUB
REPORT FOR 1966
NUMBER TWENTY
EDITED BY
P. STANDLEY

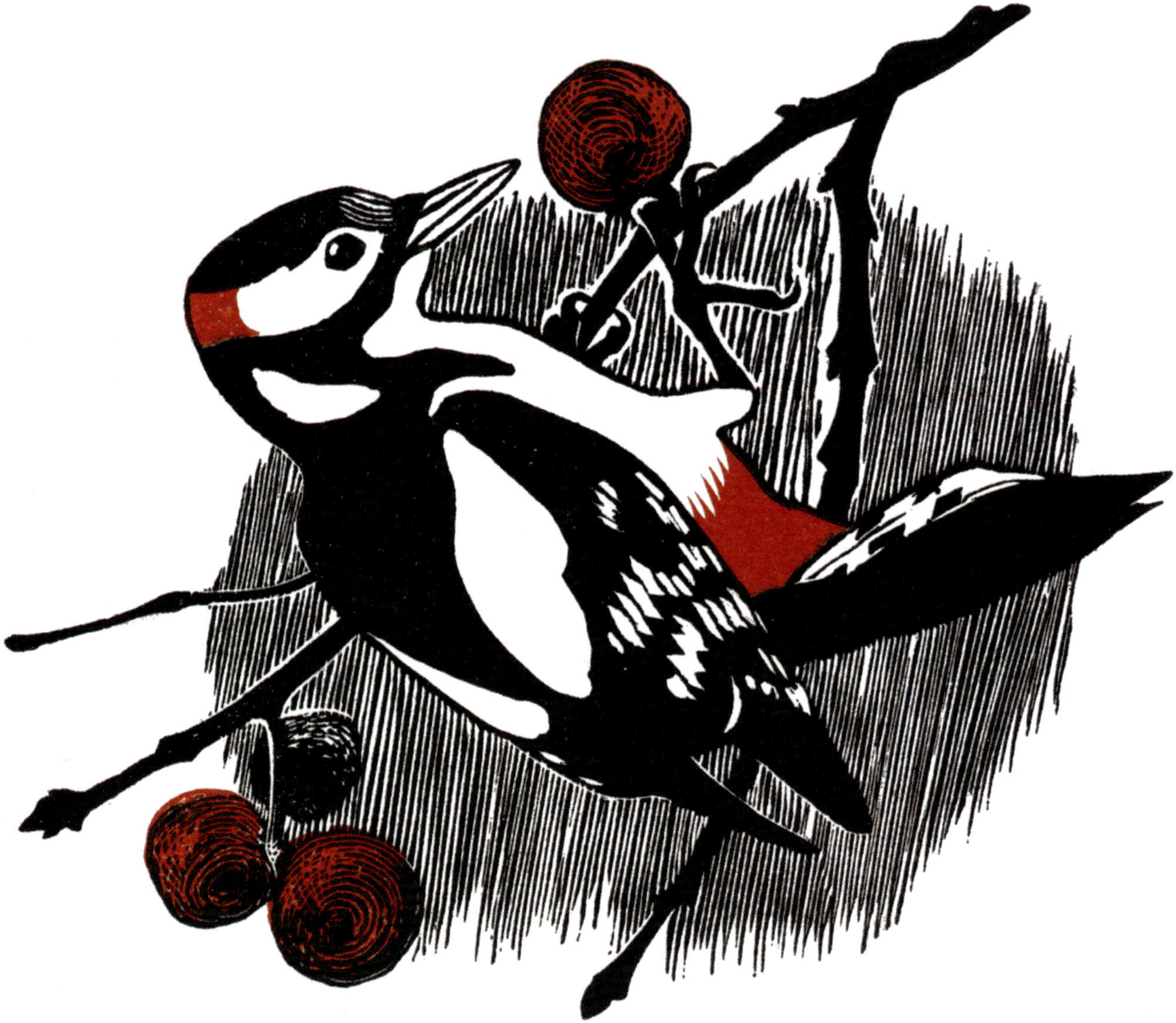

Opposite page:
ROC Report for 1955. Great Spotted Woodpecker, two-colour linocut

ROC Report for 1956. Heron, two-colour wood engraving

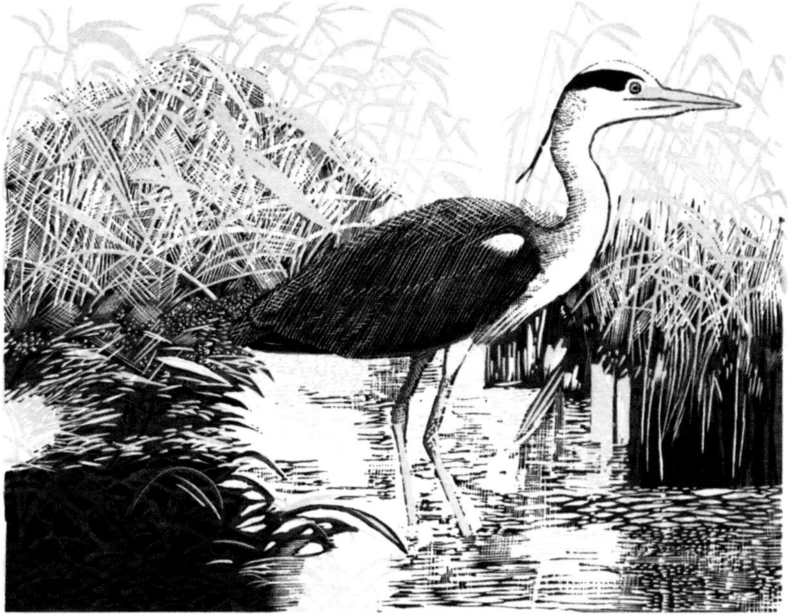

The 1954 Tufted Duck was the last cover to be printed at Sindlesham. For the next twelve years the covers were printed by Harry Stevens who, in his retirement, took on small scale printing jobs on a press in his garden shed. We established a neat, flexible typographic design, printed in two colours on a smooth grey card, and very smart they looked.

The first cover Harry printed, of a Great Spotted Woodpecker, was also the first to be printed in two colours, black and red, which probably established the second colour right from the start. The linocut illustrated something I had seen from my bedroom window, when a male woodpecker fed on the grubs in galls that had formed on the twigs of a huge oak tree in the next door garden. It hung on the twigs as acrobatically as a Blue Tit, while it attacked the galls.

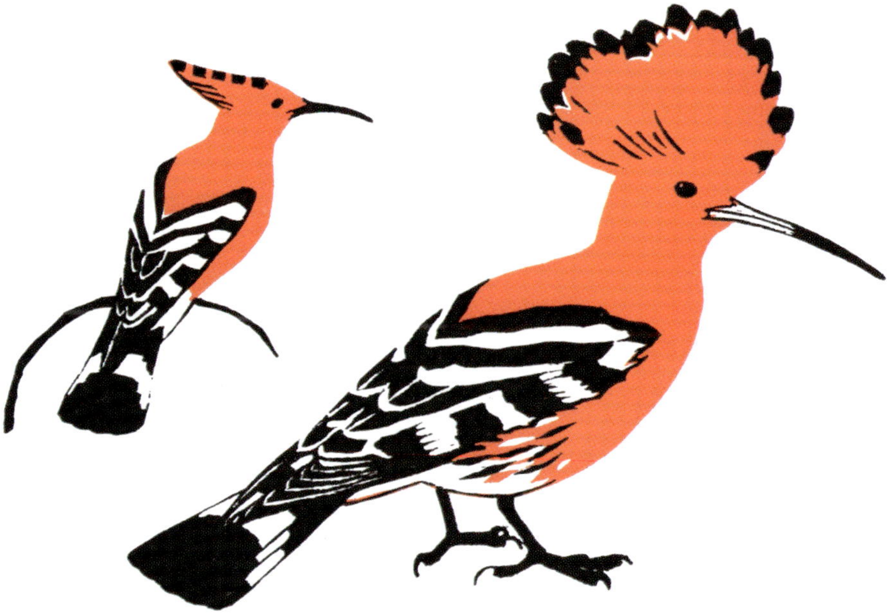

ROC Report for 1957. Hoopoe, two-colour linocut

Opposite page:
ROC Report for 1958. Stonechat, two-colour linocut and wood engraving

By the time I came to do the next cover I was a student in the Fine Art Department of Reading University and had started to try my hand at wood engraving. The design was also in two colours, black and grey, so with the title in red it meant that Harry had to put each cover through his press three times.

The next Report was back to a two-colour linocut, but the red was more orange as the subject was a Hoopoe, a not particularly rare, but an infrequent and glamorous visitor from southern Europe. If the climate really is warming it may well be a species that returns as a breeding species. Odd pairs have occasionally attempted breeding, but with no regularity. It was not a bird that I had seen myself, unlike the next species for the 1958 Report, a Stonechat: also chosen no doubt because it could be represented in the two preferred colours. This was a mix of wood engraving for the bird and lino for its chestnut chest and supporting stems.

READING ORNITHOLOGICAL CLUB

REPORT FOR 1958

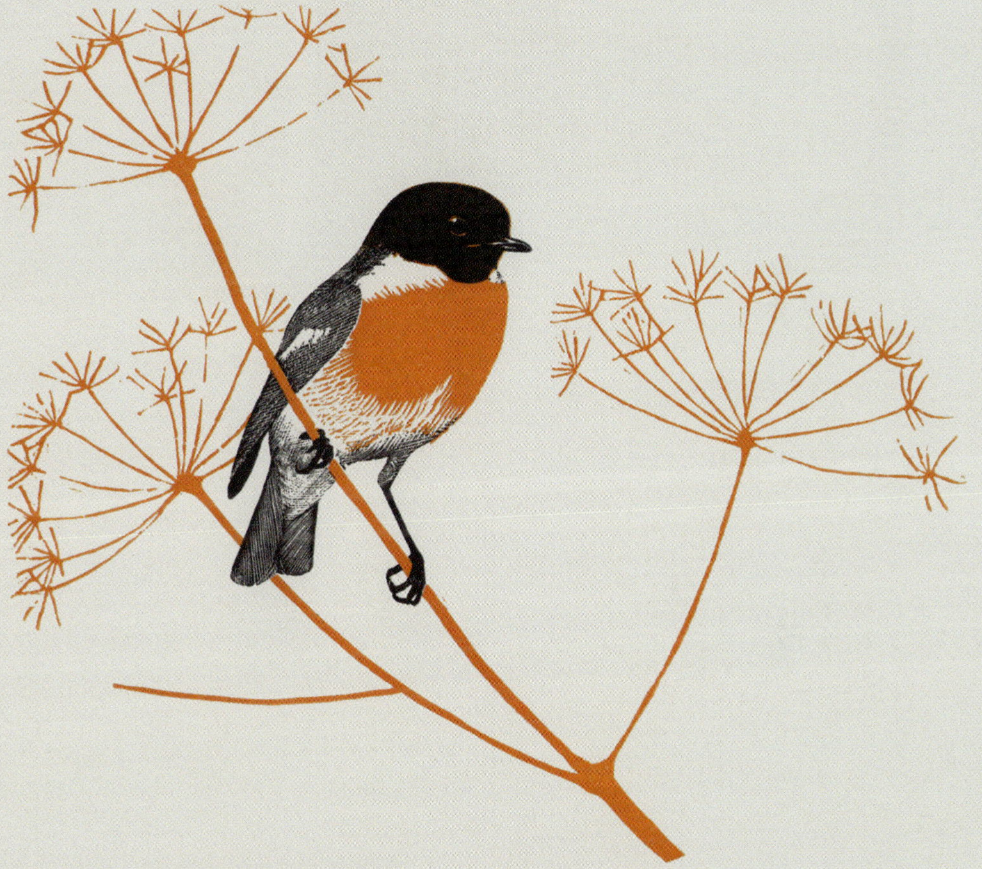

NUMBER TWELVE

EDITED BY C. C. BALCH AND N. G. B. JONES

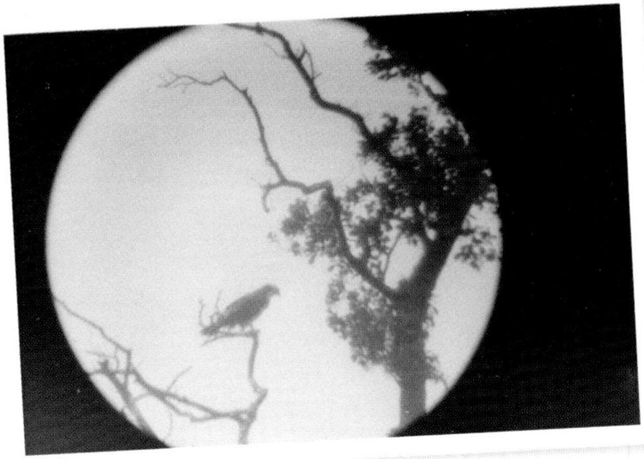

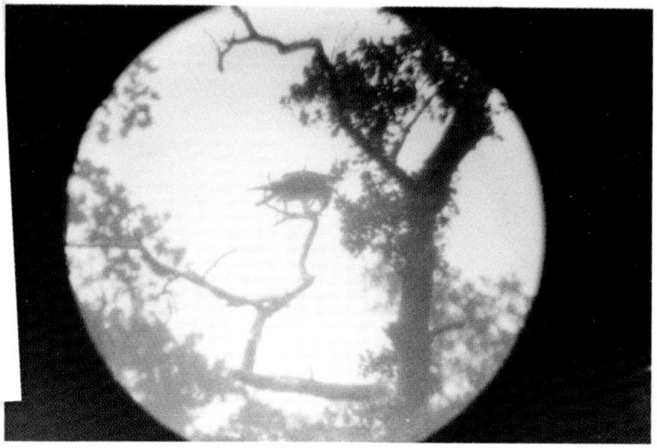

Black and white photographs taken through a telescope

Opposite page:
Sketch for 1959 report. Osprey.

ROC Report for 1959. Osprey, linocut

I had watched and sketched Stonechats on visits to Cape Clear Island, off the tip of County Cork in southern Ireland. A group from Reading, mostly from Leighton Park, had gone there in 1959 to investigate its potential for a Bird Observatory, and found that predictions of its suitability were dramatically proven to be true. It looked a promising first landing site for American birds, blown off course during their autumn migration down the east coast and carried across the Atlantic to Europe. It also turned out to be an outstandingly good spot for 'sea watching', noting the movements of seabirds around our coasts, revealing unexpectedly high numbers of birds passing offshore. It has become one of the most significant of the chain of Observatories which encircle the British and Irish islands.

On 13 September an Osprey came to Whiteknights Park Lake but only stayed around for that day. Ospreys had re-colonised Scotland in the 1950s and, with much effort on the part of conservationists, they have spread widely around Scotland and are gradually finding suitable

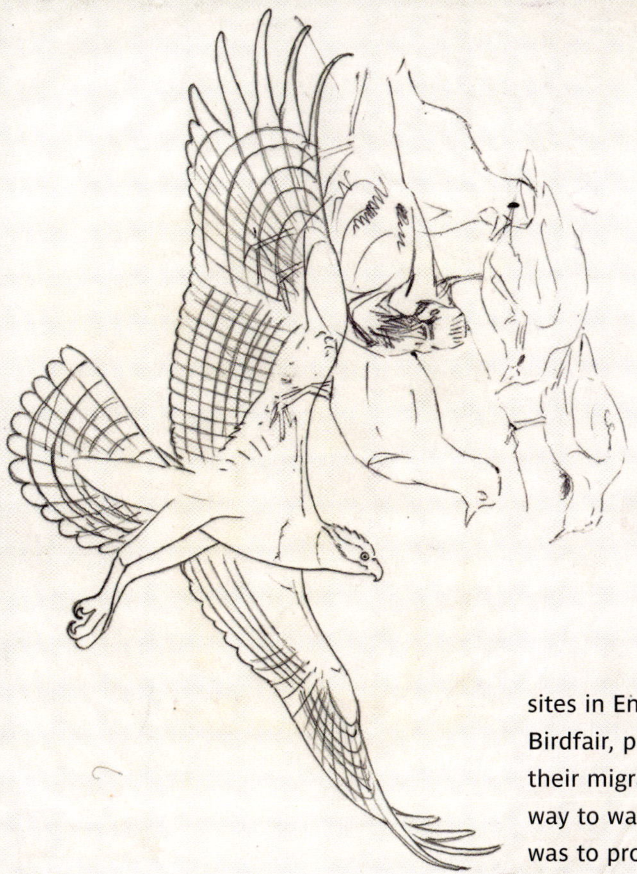

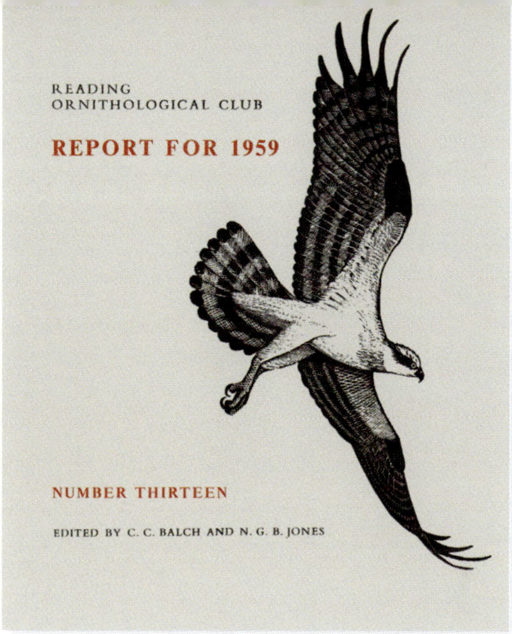

sites in England. One of these is at Rutland Water, home of the annual Birdfair, providing visitors with good views before the birds embark on their migration south. Our Reading Osprey would also have been on its way to warmer climes. I was lucky to see this unexpected visitor which was to provide the inspiration for my next linocut cover. In cutting the lino block I used wood engraving tools as well as the coarser linocutting gouges to gain finer detail on the bird's wings. At the time I was also taking black and white photographs with a very simple, almost box, camera. An indulgent uncle had passed on an old telescope, not one of the short, smart scopes that turn up at every birding twitch today, but a pull-out, long, brass affair. I couldn't see why it should be impossible to take photos through it if I held the camera lens against the eyepiece of the telescope. If I could see, why not the camera? So I had tried it out on gulls and sleeping waders on Cape Clear, and achieved results that pleased me, even if they look rather crude today – not least because the photos were circular! Today digiscoping is all the rage, and the birding

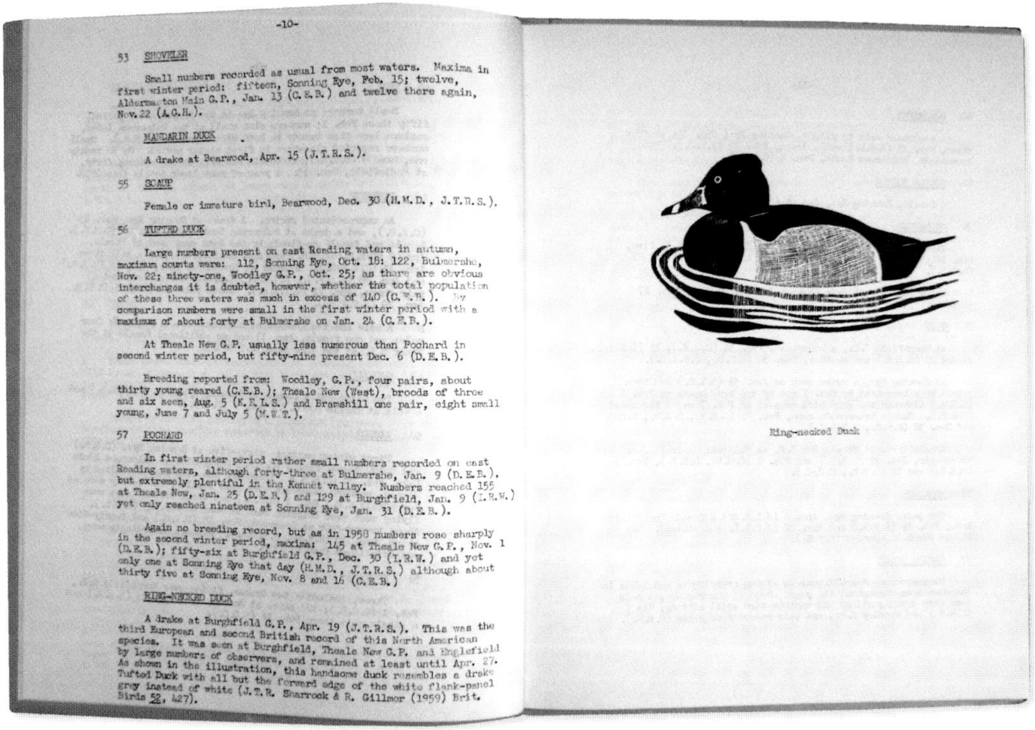

-10-

53 SHOVELER

Small numbers recorded as usual from most waters. Maxima in first winter period: fifteen, Sonning Eye, Feb. 15; twelve, Aldermaston Main G.P., Jan. 13 (C.E.B.) and twelve there again, Nov. 22 (A.G.H.).

MANDARIN DUCK

A drake at Bearwood, Apr. 15 (J.T.R.S.).

55 SCAUP

Female or immature bird, Bearwood, Dec. 30 (H.M.D., J.T.R.S.).

56 TUFTED DUCK

Large numbers present on east Reading waters in autumn, maximum counts were: 112, Sonning Eye, Oct. 18: 122, Bulmershe, Nov. 22; ninety-one, Woodley G.P., Oct. 25; as there are obvious interchanges it is doubted, however, whether the total population of these three waters was much in excess of 140 (C.E.B.). By comparison numbers were small in the first winter period with a maximum of about forty at Bulmershe on Jan. 24 (C.E.B.).

At Theale New G.P. usually less numerous than Pochard in second winter period, but fifty-nine present Dec. 6 (D.E.B.).

Breeding reported from: Woodley, G.P., four pairs, about thirty young reared (C.E.B.); Theale New (West), broods of three and six seen, Aug. 5 (K.E.L.S.) and Bramshill one pair, eight small young, June 7 and July 5 (M.W.T.).

57 POCHARD

In first winter period rather small numbers recorded on east Reading waters, although forty-three at Bulmershe, Jan. 9 (D.E.B.), but extremely plentiful in the Kennet valley. Numbers reached 155 at Theale New, Jan. 25 (D.E.B.) and 129 at Burghfield, Jan. 9 (I.R.W.) yet only reached nineteen at Sonning Eye, Jan. 31 (D.E.B.).

Again no breeding record, but as in 1958 numbers rose sharply in the second winter period, maxima: 145 at Theale New G.P., Nov. 1 (D.E.B.); fifty-six at Burghfield G.P., Dec. 30 (I.R.W.) and yet only one at Sonning Eye that day (H.M.D., J.T.R.S.) although about thirty five at Sonning Eye, Nov. 8 and 16 (C.E.B.)

RING-NECKED DUCK

A drake at Burghfield G.P., Apr. 19 (J.T.R.S.). This was the third European and second British record of this North American species. It was seen at Burghfield, Theale New G.P. and Englefield by large numbers of observers, and remained at least until Apr. 27. As shown in the illustration, this handsome duck resembles a drake Tufted Duck with all but the forward edge of the white flank-panel grey instead of white (J.T.R. Sharrock & R. Gillmor (1959) Brit. Birds 52, 427).

Ring-necked Duck

ROC Report for 1959. First ever text illustraton. Ring-necked Duck, linocut

magazines are full of remarkable work done with cameras and scopes made for each other. But this was over fifty years ago. All this ramble gives me the excuse to reproduce one of these early attempts – photographing the Osprey at Whiteknights as it perched high in a tree by the lake, feeding on a Whiteknights fish. It was a method that only worked well where birds were stationary. I would aim and focus the telescope which was clipped to a short shooter's stand. In order carefully to manoeuvre the camera to fit the lens over the eyepiece, and release the shutter, I had to take my eye from the scope. This meant that I could not watch the bird at the same time, so occasionally I photographed a tail as the uncooperative model left the scene.

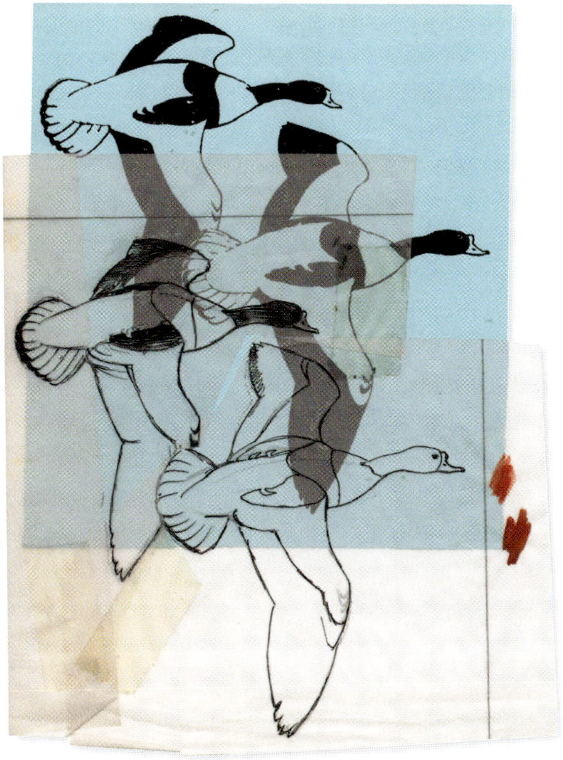

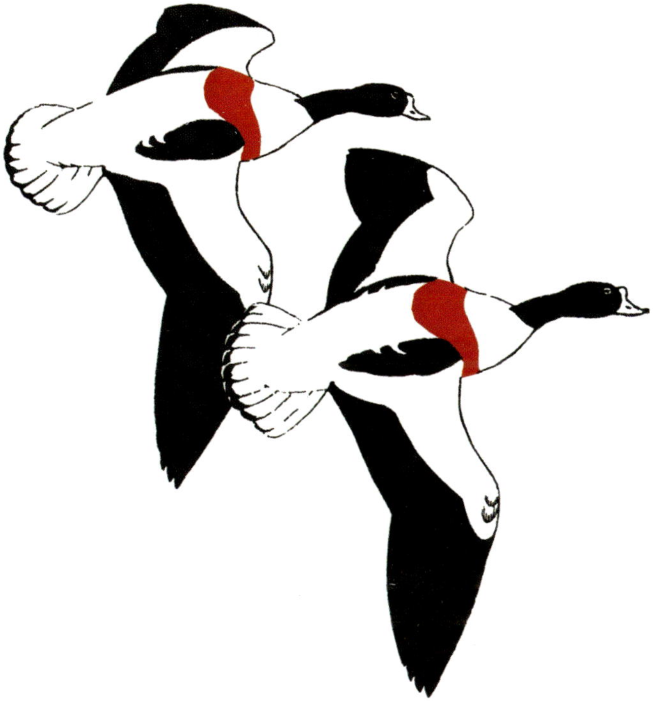

Sketch and proof of black lino block for 1960 report. Shelducks

ROC Report for 1960. Shelducks, two-colour linocut

The 1959 Report also included a linocut inside, 'commemorating our rarest bird ever with our first text illustration.' The drake Ring-necked Duck, found by Tim Sharrock at Burghfield Gravel Pit on 19 April, was the third European and second British record. This American diving duck is found right across North America to Alaska. It had presumably been blown off its spring route north, travelling from winter quarters in South and Central America. It stayed for over a week and was seen by large numbers of bird watchers. I even photographed it through my telescope!

Finding two-colour birds, preferably black and red(ish) was not difficult, and when Shelducks dropped into one of the gravel pits in February 1960 they gave me a perfect cover subject. A Shelduck is, from a distance,

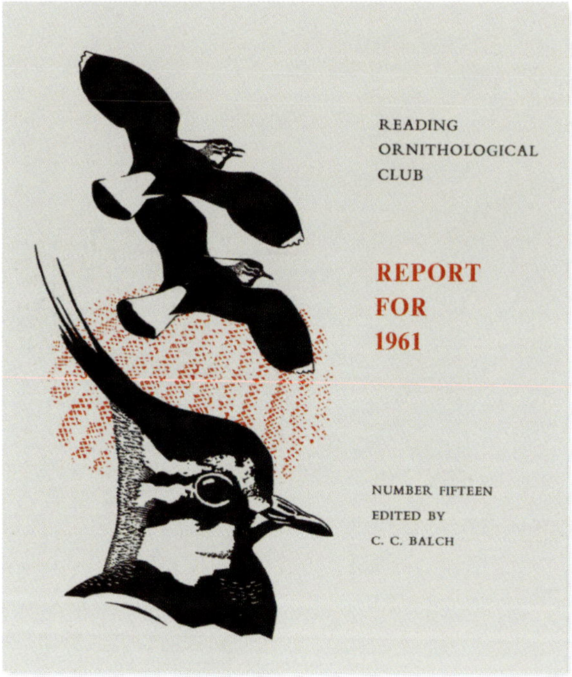

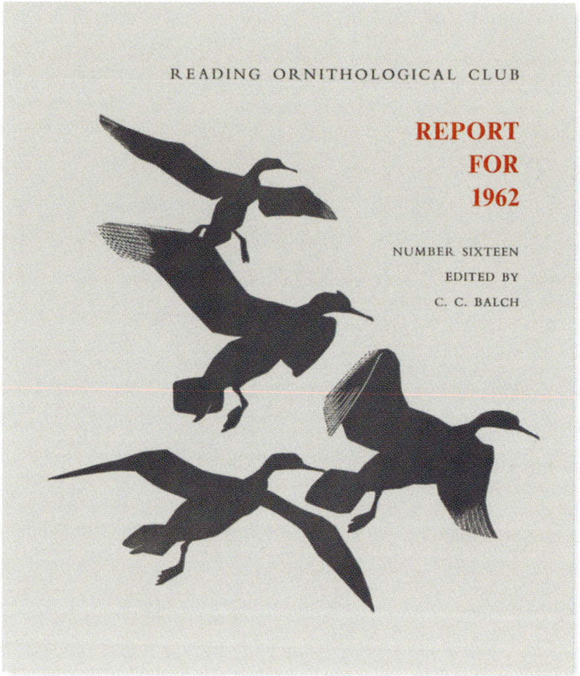

ROC Report for 1961. Lapwings, two-colour linocut

ROC Report for 1962. Shags, linocut

Opposite page:
Clipping from the *Reading Standard*, April 1962

black and white with a wide terracotta orange band around its chest. A closer view shows the red bill and pink legs and a rich, green sheen adds lustre to its black head and neck.

With no really special bird in 1961, I made a linocut of one of my favourite birds, the Lapwing: another bird which also appears black and white, but a good view, in bright sunlight, makes it obvious why it was once called the Green Plover. Although they also have warm undertail coverts, I chose to use the second colour on a section of ploughed field in the background.

The ornithological event of 1962, already described in *Birds, Blocks and Stamps* (2012), was the arrival, after an easterly gale, of a flock of over 30 shags which landed on the Thames near Kennet mouth, staying

... be profitable.

If services are essential to the community some way must be found to keep them going, by subsidy or by allowing, as Sir Anthony suggested, small operators to came in.

... connected. Luckily, Loppy wasn't hurt, despite the drop."

... Wesley Maughan for a fitness test this morning.

All shopkeepers are invited to attend. At the same meeting the ...

Day early

EASTER next week. The "Reading Standard" will be published a day early, on Thursday morning. Advertisers and correspondents please send your copy in early.

FLEW FROM FINLAND

A black headed gull, found dead in Reading in February, had, it was discovered this week, flown here from Finland—a distance of nearly 1,200 miles. The bird had been ringed at Helsinki last June.

They came to see the "wreck"

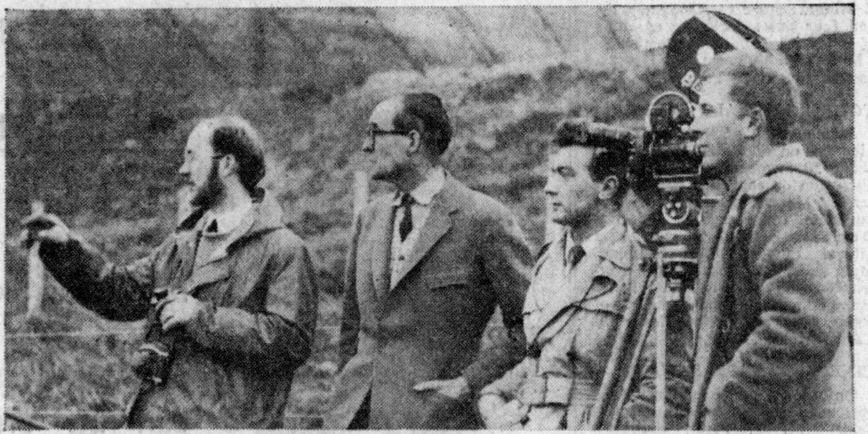

[Photo: Jeffrey Taylor, ARPS

A BBC TV camera unit, headed by Macdonald Hastings, visited Reading this week to make a film of the shags—featured in the *Reading Standard* three weeks ago—that have been on the Thames since the beginning of March. The film, which was shown on the "Tonight" programme on Wednesday, included shots, taken from a boat, of 24 shags on the bank, swimming and diving in the river and, finally, a sequence of the birds flying to roost on the gasholders. The cameraman was Geoffrey Mulligan, who has accompanied David Attenborough on two of his "Zoo Quest" expeditions.

Macdonald Hastings was filmed interviewing Robert Gillmor (left), secretary of the Reading Ornithological Club, who told him about the extensive "wreck" of these sea birds which are so rarely seen inland. The Reading flock, which had numbered over 30, was the largest recorded in over 20 counties.

DOCTOR FINED £150 AND BANNED FROM DRIVING

13. 4. 62

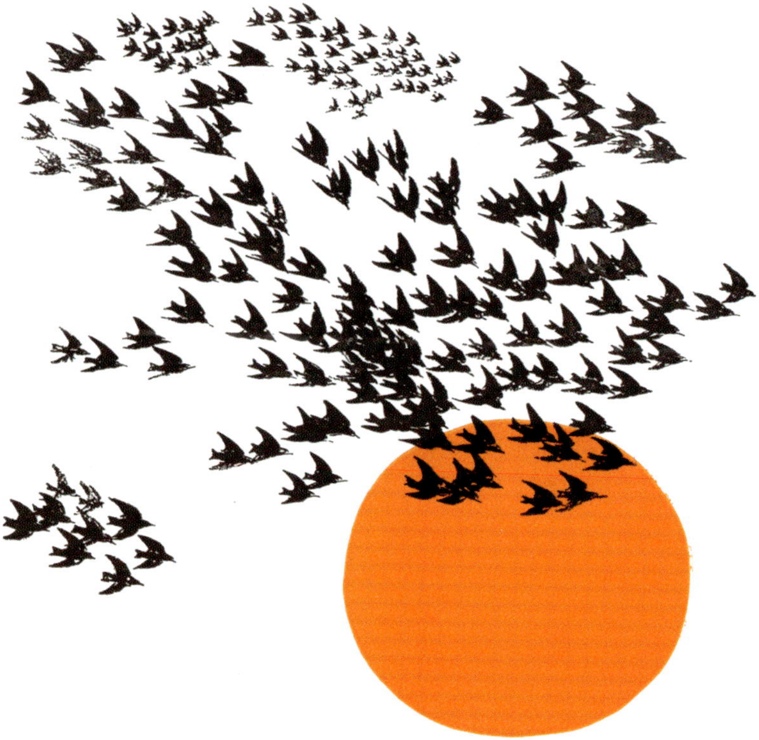

ROC Report for 1963. Starlings, two-colour linocut and brush drawing

there for the next two months. Their evening flight from the river, circling up to descend on the nearest Reading has to cliffs, the gas holders, became a regular spectacle, encouraged by their appearance on the popular evening TV show 'Tonight'. My linocut shows a group, silhouetted in grey, coming in to land on the railing encircling the top of the gasometers.

In the early sixties the vast housing estates of Maiden Erleigh, on the east side of Reading, were hardly a gleam in the planners' eyes. Duncan Wood had taken us, on our bicycles, during a Friday evening Bird Group, to see Red-backed Shrikes nesting in rough ground, now covered by bricks, mortar and concrete. This was once a common breeding species, but since the early 1960s there has been a dramatic decline and it is now a rare passage migrant. The reasons for this are unclear, but habitat loss must surely play a big part. At Bulmershe there was an extensive lake, surrounded by woodlands; and in the autumn of 1962 these woods became the site of a huge Starling roost with up to 250,000 birds. It was a truly remarkable experience to stand at the lakeside and watch the vast flock grow as parties flew in from all directions to perform their aerial ballet against the setting sun. Gradually, as it grew dark, the birds would peel off and gather in the tops of beech trees, before flowing down to roost in the Rhododendron bushes below. Here, the noise and smell was incredible as they jostled for space. I was inspired to do several versions of the remarkable scene: a large linocut print, a book illustration and, of course, a ROC Report cover, combining a brush drawing of the Starlings and a linocut sun. The large linocut was eventually used on the cover of *BIRDS,* the RSPB members' magazine, although not originally designed for the purpose. The editor, Nick Hammond, made an anxious phone call to say that a cover he had commissioned had arrived, but could not be used. Had I anything suitable to save the day? The Starling roost was the right shape so off it went, post haste, and became my sixth of twelve covers for the magazine.

For the 1964 cover I returned to line drawing on scraperboard, this time of a group of five immature Bewick's Swans seen at Manor Farm from 8 February to 24 March. These were probably on their way back to their breeding grounds in the Arctic, having wintered in the west, perhaps at the Wildfowl and Wetlands Trust reserve at Slimbridge in Gloucestershire, where large numbers spend the winter. They are named after the great eighteenth-century wood engraver Thomas Bewick, who wrote and illustrated the first 'field guide', his *History of British Birds*. Scraperboard is a thin card with a hard smooth plaster coating. It can be drawn on with pen and ink, and brush for filling in areas of black or

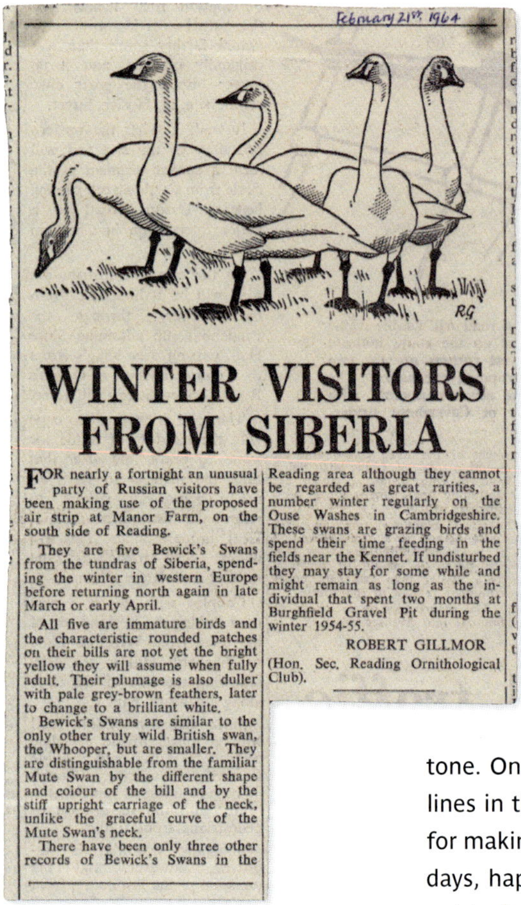
February 21st 1964

WINTER VISITORS FROM SIBERIA

FOR nearly a fortnight an unusual party of Russian visitors have been making use of the proposed air strip at Manor Farm, on the south side of Reading.

They are five Bewick's Swans from the tundras of Siberia, spending the winter in western Europe before returning north again in late March or early April.

All five are immature birds and the characteristic rounded patches on their bills are not yet the bright yellow they will assume when fully adult. Their plumage is also duller with pale grey-brown feathers, later to change to a brilliant white.

Bewick's Swans are similar to the only other truly wild British swan, the Whooper, but are smaller. They are distinguishable from the familiar Mute Swan by the different shape and colour of the bill and by the stiff upright carriage of the neck, unlike the graceful curve of the Mute Swan's neck.

There have been only three other records of Bewick's Swans in the Reading area although they cannot be regarded as great rarities, a number winter regularly on the Ouse Washes in Cambridgeshire. These swans are grazing birds and spend their time feeding in the fields near the Kennet. If undisturbed they may stay for some while and might remain as long as the individual that spent two months at Burghfield Gravel Pit during the winter 1954-55.

ROBERT GILLMOR

(Hon. Sec. Reading Ornithological Club).

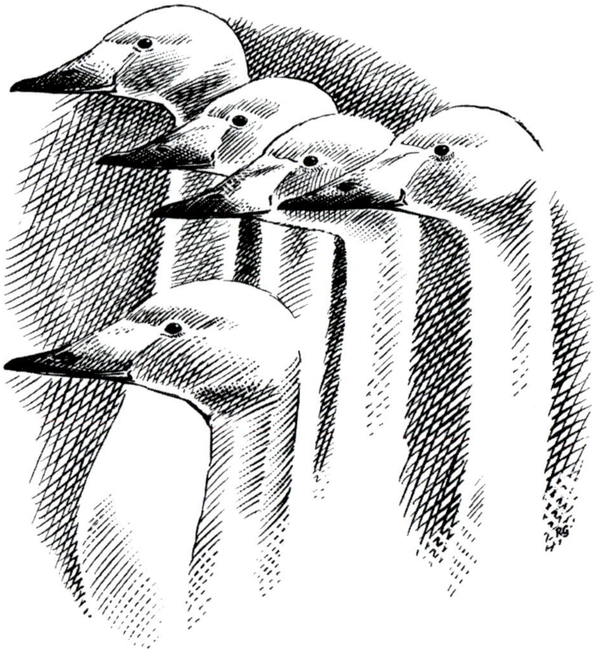

Clipping from the *Berkshire Chronicle*, February 1964

ROC Report for 1964. Bewick's Swans, scraperboard

tone. Once the ink is dry a sharp scraping tool will produce fine white lines in the black, with other tools for thicker marks. It is also splendid for making corrections! I have used white scraperboard from my earliest days, happier with it than the black board which requires rather different techniques. One of the masters of the art of scraperboard who influenced me was Charles Tunnicliffe who must have done thousands in a lifetime of illustrating. He was one of the most prolific illustrators of the twentieth century, and an expert engraver and watercolourist. He was the only artist specialising in wildlife subjects to be elected to the Royal Academy. He filled sketchbook after sketchbook with his observations of the birds around his home on Anglesey, and could turn his hand to any country subject that his publisher required. Many of my own scraperboards have very little scraping, just enough to lighten some crosshatching or add a highlight or thin a line. But the very act of drawing on the board has its particular effect on the lines and textures produced. I reported the presence of the Bewick's Swans in a short piece for the *Berkshire Chronicle*, which also reproduced another scraperboard of the quintet.

While Harry Stevens could print directly from my lino or woodblocks, pen and ink drawings and scraperboards had to be taken to the Reading Process Engraving Company. Here they would be enlarged or reduced as required, usually the latter, and turned into a metal printing plate. This involved photography and etching in an acid bath. I would cycle down Cressingham Hill and hand my drawing to Mr Mott – always clad in long, brown overalls. The gleaming new block would be ready for collection a couple of days later, along with two perfect proofs on shiny paper, which I treasured!

The next cover was based on another personal observation, this time near the old Reading Sewage Farm, off the Bath Road. This had been a great birding area in its prime which, sadly, was rather before my time, although a place we looked at regularly as there was usually something worth seeing. On this occasion in September 1965, in the evening light, a Heron and a Short-eared Owl were clearly not happy to be sharing the same air space. My report described how they were 'seen flying in slow, tight circles around each other, in view for about a mile, 200ft up. The Heron (a juvenile) made stoops and lunges at the owl and called occasionally. The owl apparently made no attempt to break off the encounter.' I cycled home and made drawings from memory and turned these into the cover drawing. This was done on a rough watercolour paper, using a black Chinagraph pencil which makes a thickish, greasy black line. The pencil can be worked across the paper to pick up and bring out its grainy texture and is black enough to be held in the process of producing the metal printing plate. The finished drawing is softer than that made by straight pen and ink, and it is fun to look for papers with

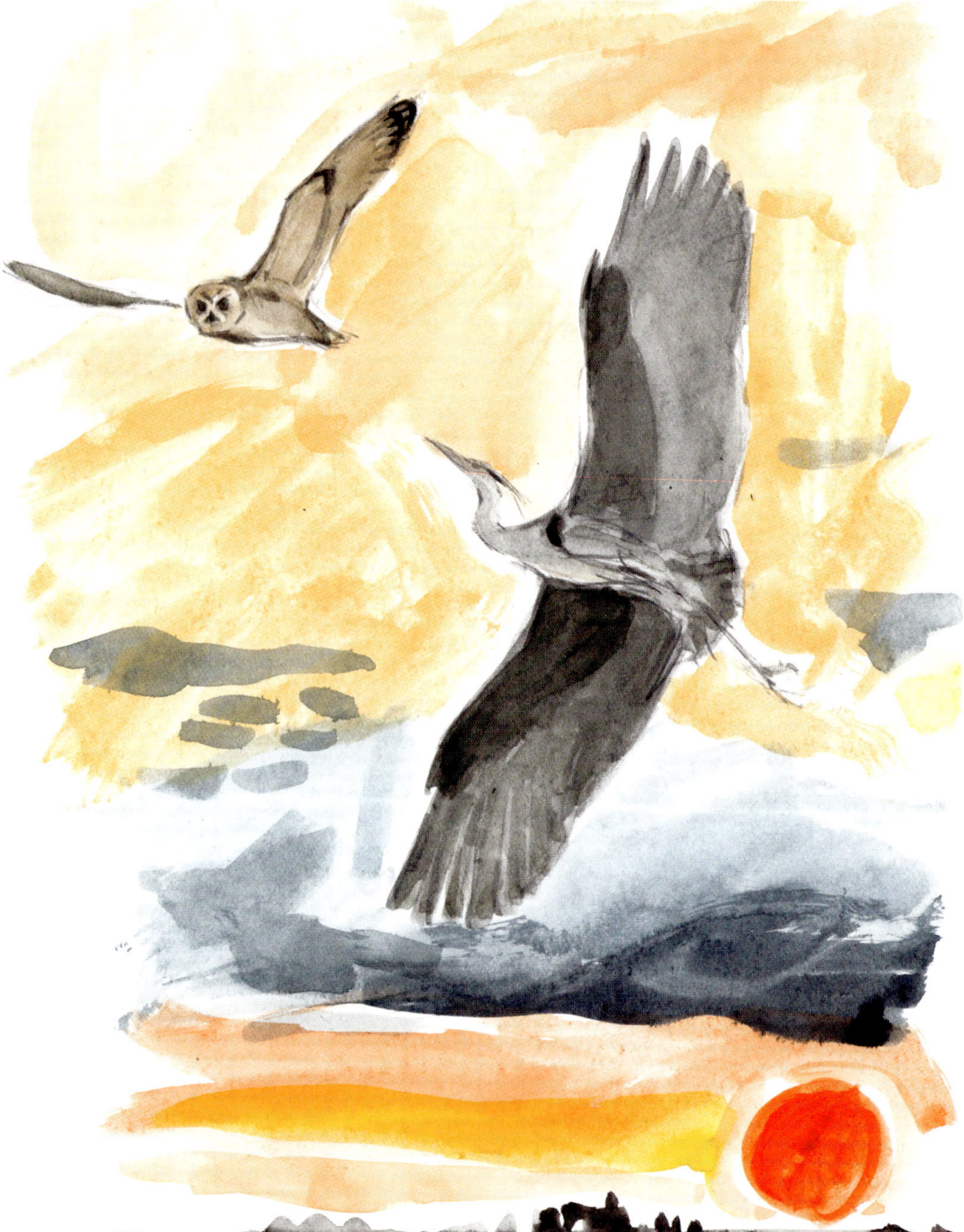

Opposite page:
Sketch for 1965 report. Heron and Short-eared Owl

ROC Report for 1966. Waxwings, line drawing

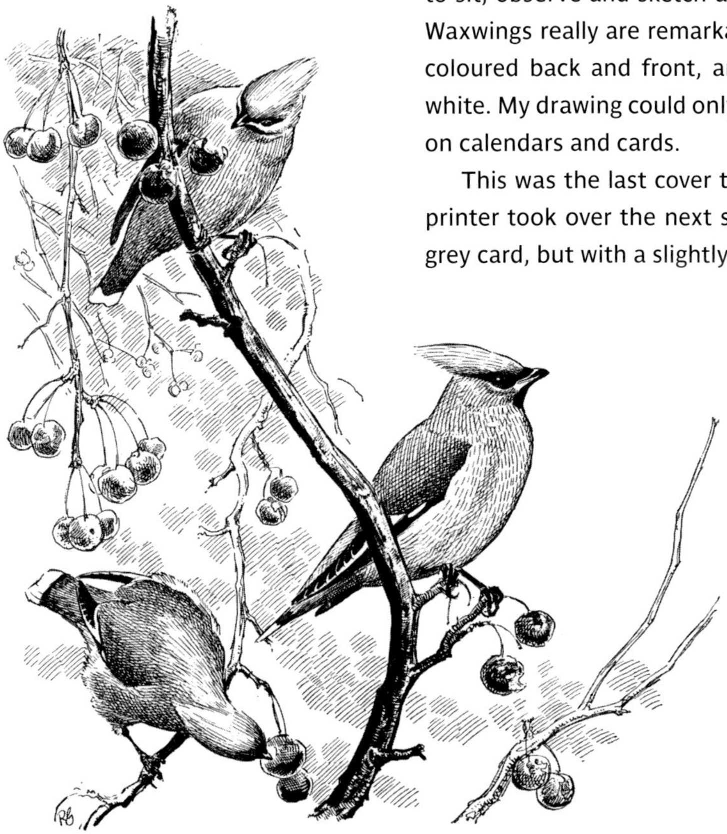

different textures to work on. Some wrapping materials, never destined for the studio, can be just what is required.

Some years are noted as 'Waxwing years' when this handsome, Starling-sized Scandinavian arrives in considerable numbers to lay waste berry-bearing shrubs in gardens, town centres and the countryside generally. Two doors down the avenue from us was just such a garden, with a large crab apple laden with small ripe fruits. A gang of Waxwings found this much to their liking and settled to ransack its bounty. Our neighbour's bedroom overlooked the site of this invasion and I was welcome to sit, observe and sketch as I wished. And I certainly wished! Close up, Waxwings really are remarkable with their incredibly smooth, delicately coloured back and front, and sharp accents of black, red, yellow and white. My drawing could only be in black but I did other paintings for use on calendars and cards.

This was the last cover to be printed by Harry Stevens, and another printer took over the next seven covers, retaining the basic layout and grey card, but with a slightly different typeface.

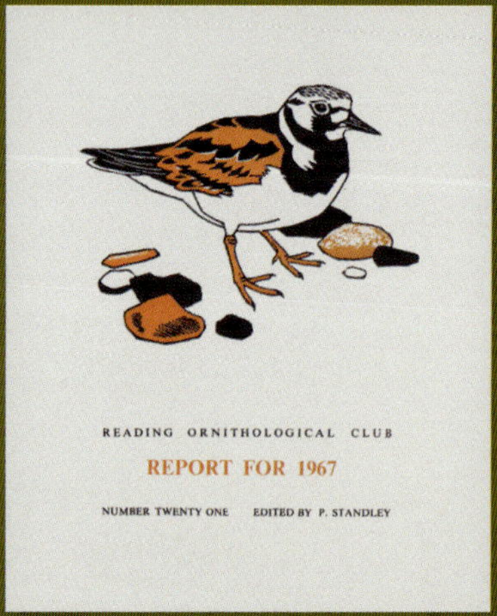
READING ORNITHOLOGICAL CLUB
REPORT FOR 1967
NUMBER TWENTY ONE EDITED BY P. STANDLEY

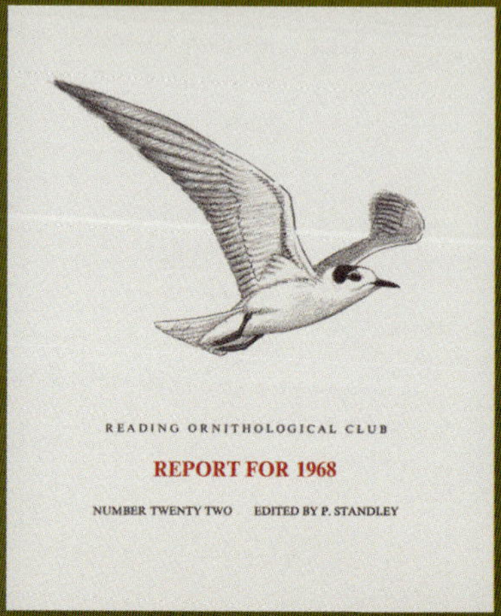
READING ORNITHOLOGICAL CLUB
REPORT FOR 1968
NUMBER TWENTY TWO EDITED BY P. STANDLEY

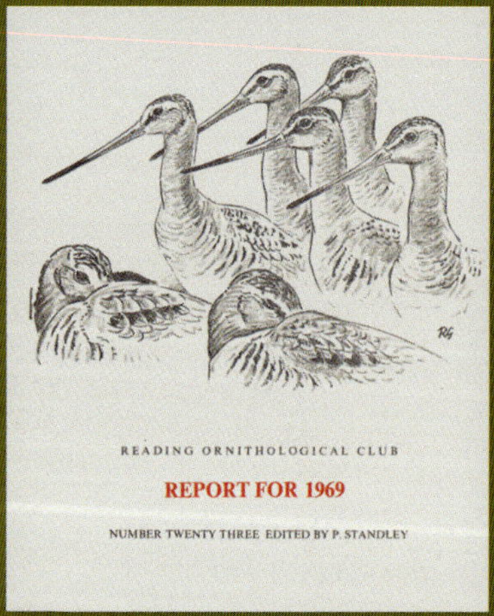
READING ORNITHOLOGICAL CLUB
REPORT FOR 1969
NUMBER TWENTY THREE EDITED BY P. STANDLEY

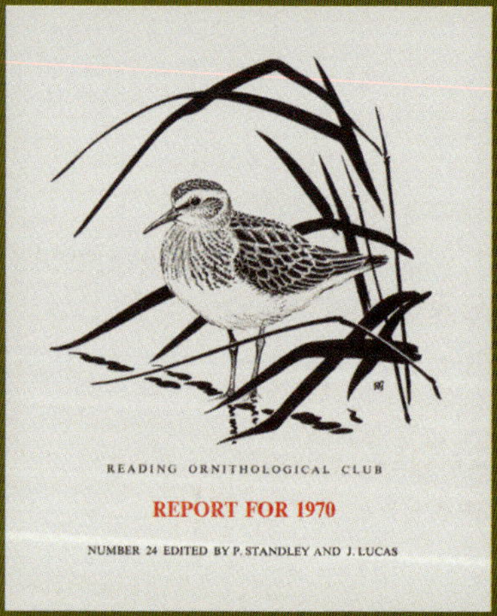
READING ORNITHOLOGICAL CLUB
REPORT FOR 1970
NUMBER 24 EDITED BY P. STANDLEY AND J. LUCAS

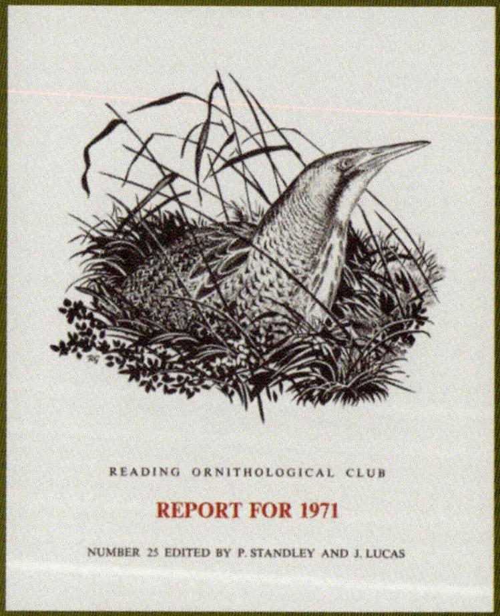
READING ORNITHOLOGICAL CLUB
REPORT FOR 1971
NUMBER 25 EDITED BY P. STANDLEY AND J. LUCAS

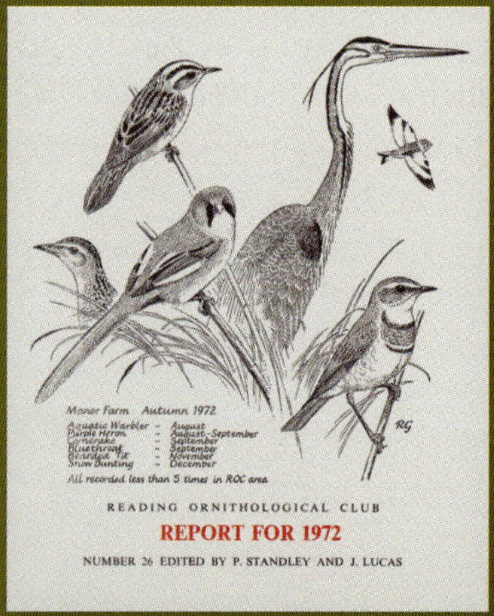
Manor Farm Autumn 1972
Aquatic Warbler - August
Purple Heron - August-September
Corncrake - September
Bluethroat - September
Bearded Tit - November
Snow Bunting - December
All recorded less than 5 times in ROC area
READING ORNITHOLOGICAL CLUB
REPORT FOR 1972
NUMBER 26 EDITED BY P. STANDLEY AND J. LUCAS

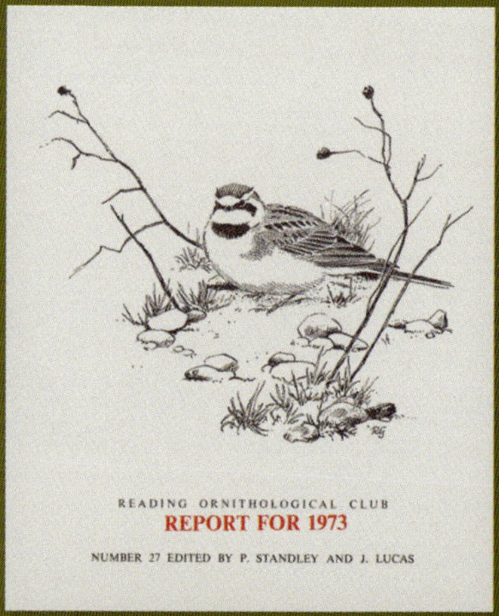
READING ORNITHOLOGICAL CLUB
REPORT FOR 1973
NUMBER 27 EDITED BY P. STANDLEY AND J. LUCAS

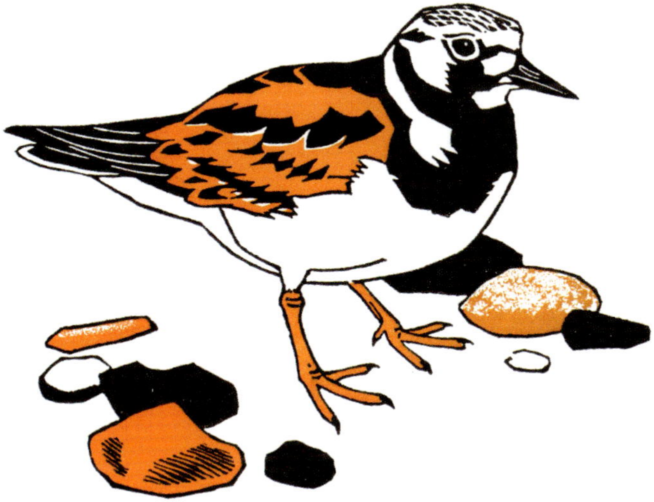

ROC Report for 1967. Turnstone, two-colour linocut

It was back to a two-colour linocut for the Turnstone on the 1967 cover. In full spring plumage this is a most handsome wader with black head and chest markings, rich brown upper parts and orange legs. Turnstones had arrived at Theale Gravel Pit in early May, and the three seen there on 8 May was the highest number recorded since eight were sighted at Manor Farm in 1932.

In 1969 I made my first trip to the USA during which I visited a number of the leading American bird artists. One of these, Al Gilbert, a young artist rapidly making a name for himself, introduced me to coquille board which he used to great effect in his black and white illustrations. The year before had seen the publication of *The Audubon Illustrated Handbook of American Birds*, a heavy tome of over 500 pages and full of Al's coquille board drawings. It is a thin white card with different embossed textures on either side. The Chinagraph pencil works brilliantly on this board, which is also smooth and takes pen and ink extremely well. Many future covers, especially those done in the mid-seventies and

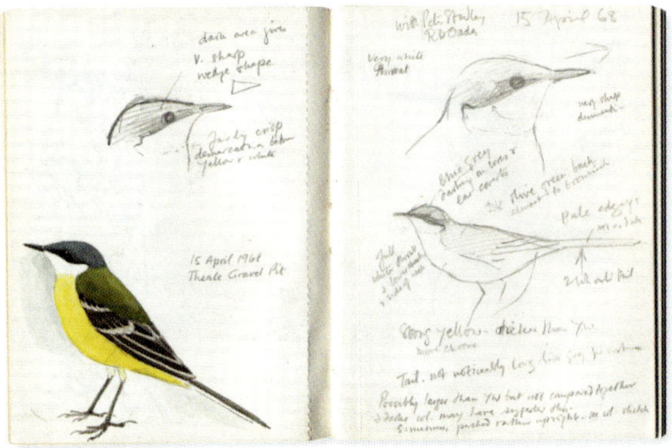

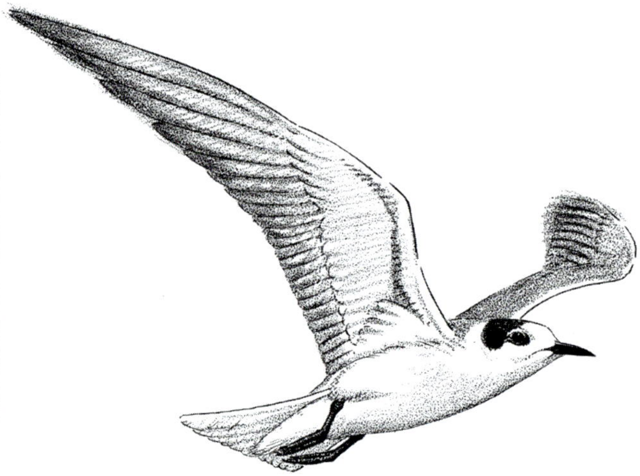

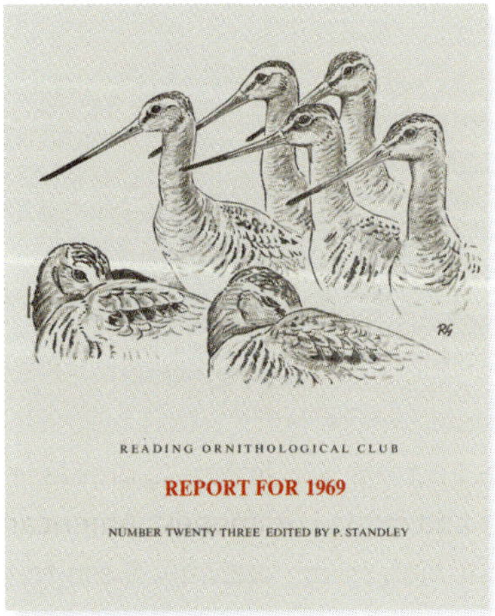

early eighties, were drawn on this board. Al kindly acquired a quantity for me as I could not find it in this country. I subsequently used it a great deal for general illustrating along with scraperboard. The textures were often more suitable than crosshatching and were especially good for drawing mammals where an even tone was required to suggest, for example, the fine pelt of a Fox or Rabbit.

The White-winged Black Tern was the first cover drawn on coquille board. It had turned up on 27 October at Theale Gravel Pit, only the second record for Berkshire. Since then there have been further records of this rare passage migrant from eastern Europe. Had the cover been in full colour there might have been competition from a gorgeous Ashy-headed Wagtail, which I watched with two members of the club on 15 April. From my notes and sketches I made this full colour drawing. The report noted: 'It remained to breed with a female Yellow Wagtail rearing six young (half-grown on June 1st) and possibly attempted a second brood.'

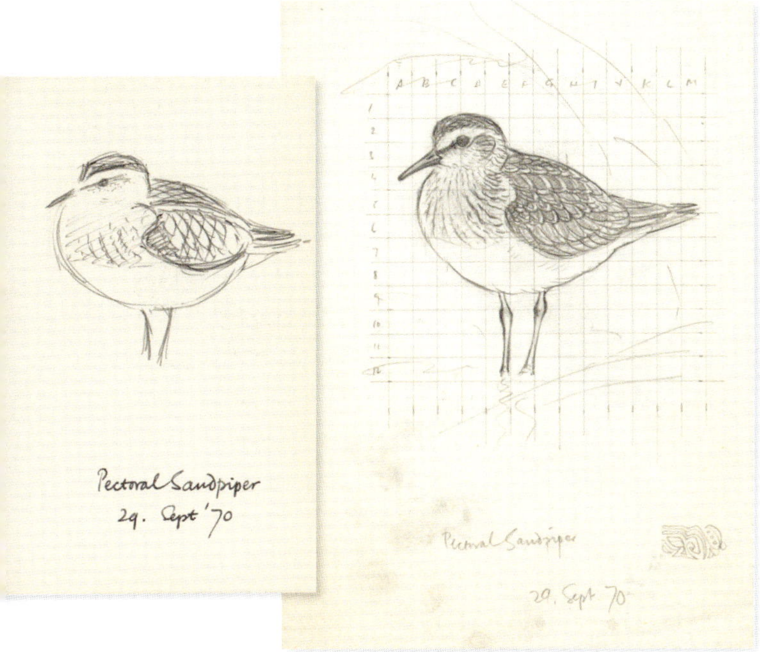

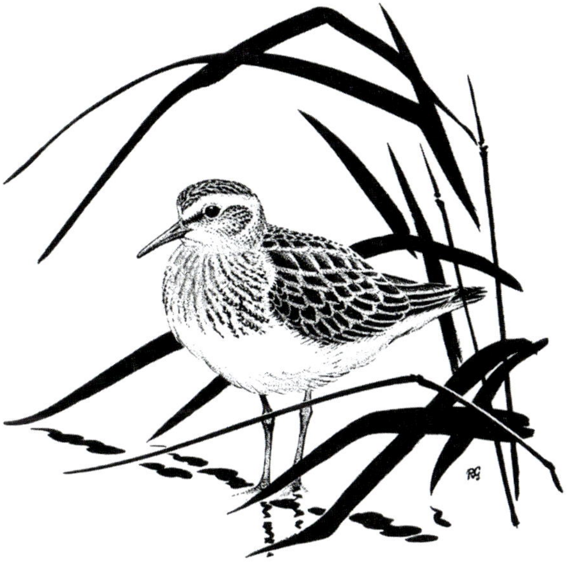

ROC Report for 1972. Pectoral Sandpiper, line drawing on coquille board

Opposite page:
Sketch of Ashy-headed Wagtail, 1968

ROC Report for 1968. White-winged Black Tern, line drawing on coquille board

ROC Report for 1969. Black-tailed Godwits, line drawing on coquille board

The Black-tailed Godwits on the 1969 cover were at Manor Farm for several days in the spring and I saw seven there on 28 March.

Another wader, and a proper rarity as it was the first American wader to be seen in the ROC area, was a Pectoral Sandpiper. It breeds in North America and north-east Siberia and is the commonest American vagrant to Britain, most often, like our bird, in the autumn. Despite a number of unusual records in 1970 this was the one chosen to grace our cover. Here I had some fun with a full brush of black ink, and a somewhat oriental flourish in drawing the foliage around the Sandpiper.

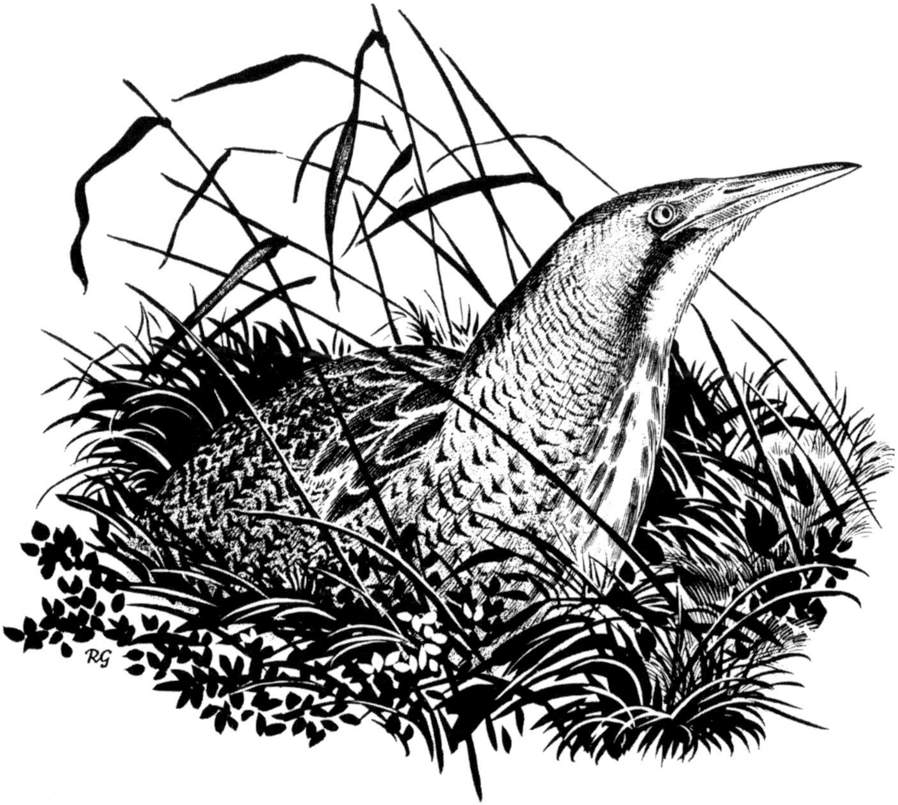

ROC Report for 1971. Bittern, line drawing on coquille board

There was more brush work in the drawing of a Bittern for the 1971 cover, as it stalks slowly through the vegetation. Bitterns bred regularly in Berkshire until the late eighteenth century, then becoming scarce visitors, but are now seen annually, usually during the winter months.

The Report for 1972 gave me the chance to make a change from the usual single species. There had been a number of rarities at Manor Farm and it seemed a good idea to illustrate six of them, although scale was a bit of a problem.

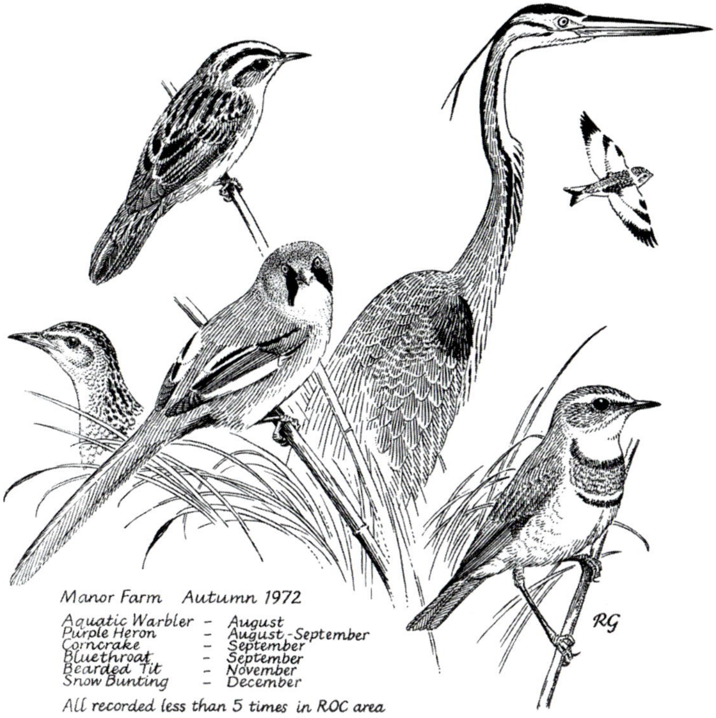

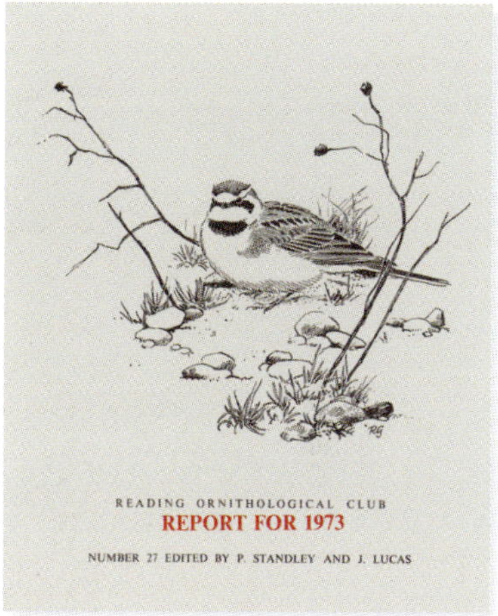

ROC Report for 1972. Six varieties at Manor Farm (Aquatic Warbler, Purple Heron, Corncrake, Bluethroat, Bearded Tit, and Snow Bunting), line drawing on coquille board

ROC Report for 1973. Shorelark, line drawing

The 1973 Shore Lark had been found at Theale Gravel Pit in December – another Berkshire first. Nowadays, during the winter, I can sometimes see these delightful winter visitors from Scandinavia on our pebbly north Norfolk beach within a ten minute walk of the house, often in the company of Snow Buntings. Today I would make more of the head pattern of black and lemon yellow and head tufts which are unique to this attractive species and account for its other name – Horned Lark. This cover, printed by the Goodwin Press in London, brought to an end, after a quarter of a century, the duplicated report, stapled into its thin card cover.

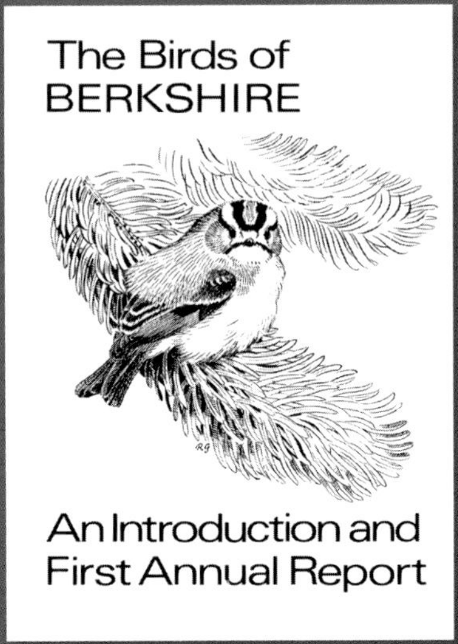
The Birds of
BERKSHIRE
RG
An Introduction and
First Annual Report

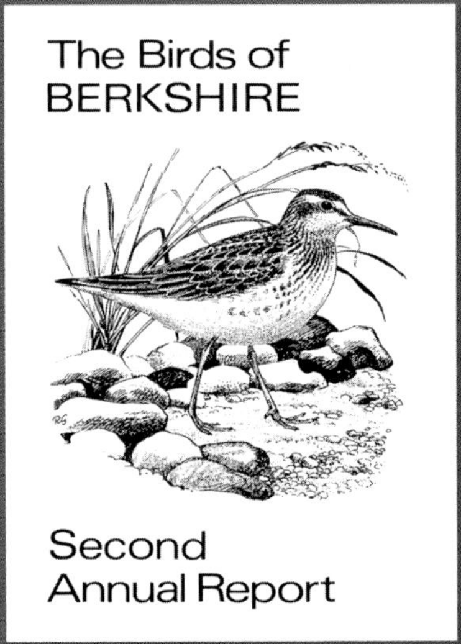
The Birds of
BERKSHIRE
RG
Second
Annual Report

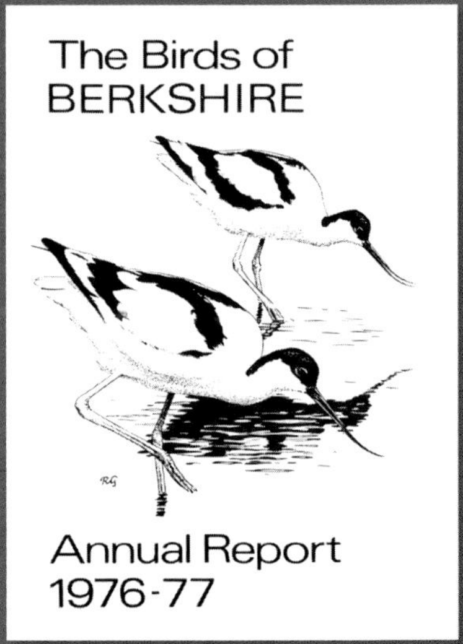
The Birds of
BERKSHIRE
RG
Annual Report
1976-77

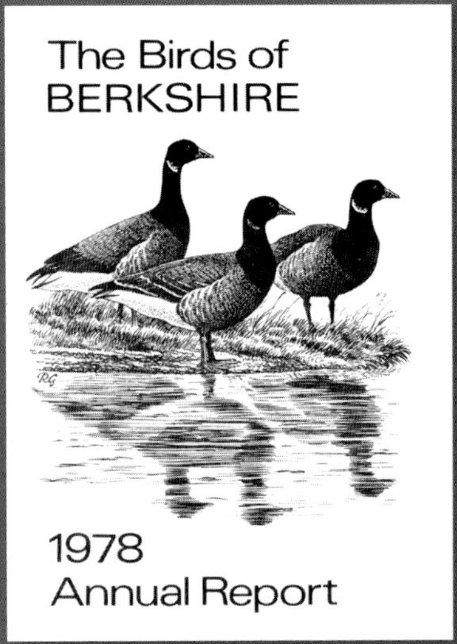
The Birds of
BERKSHIRE
RG
1978
Annual Report

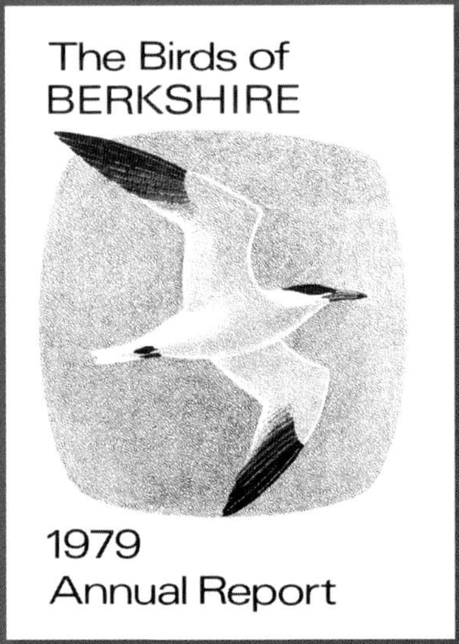
The Birds of
BERKSHIRE
1979
Annual Report

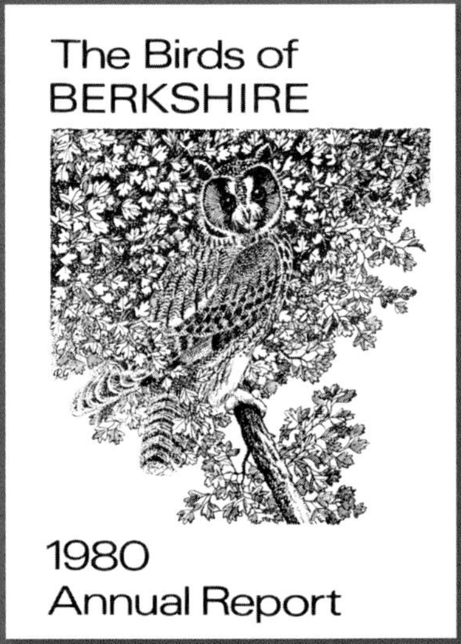
The Birds of
BERKSHIRE
RG
1980
Annual Report

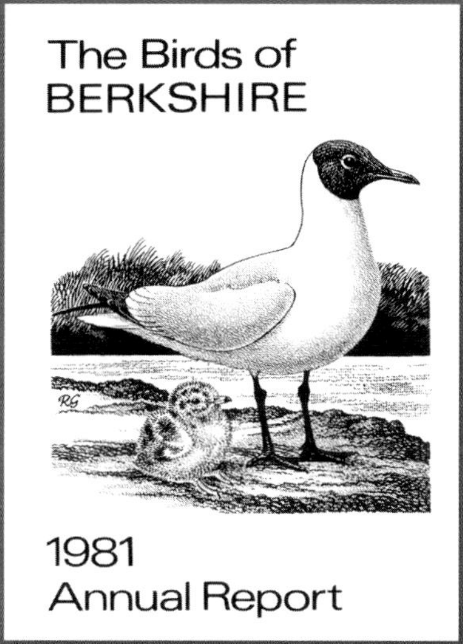
The Birds of
BERKSHIRE
RG
1981
Annual Report

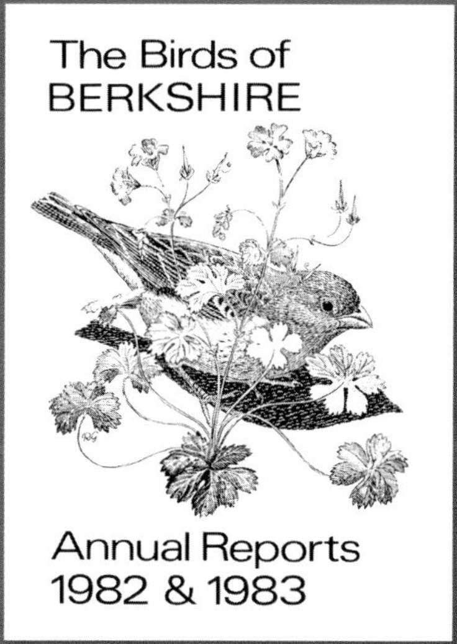
The Birds of
BERKSHIRE
Annual Reports
1982 & 1983

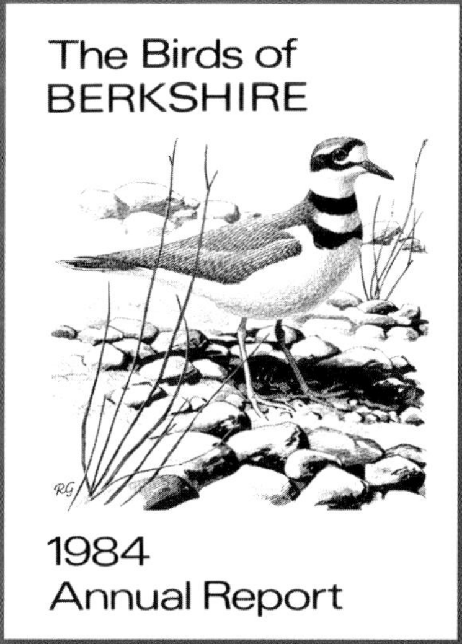
The Birds of
BERKSHIRE
RG
1984
Annual Report

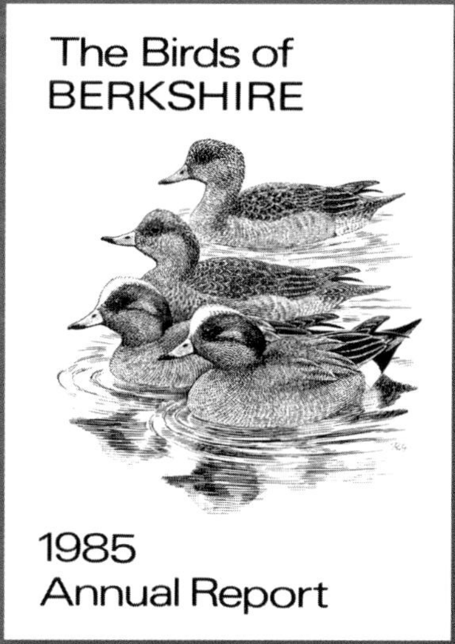
The Birds of
BERKSHIRE
1985
Annual Report

The Birds of Berkshire 1974. Firecrest, line & brush on scraperboard

Opposite page:
The Birds of Berkshire 1975. Sharp-tailed Sandpiper, line drawing on coquille board

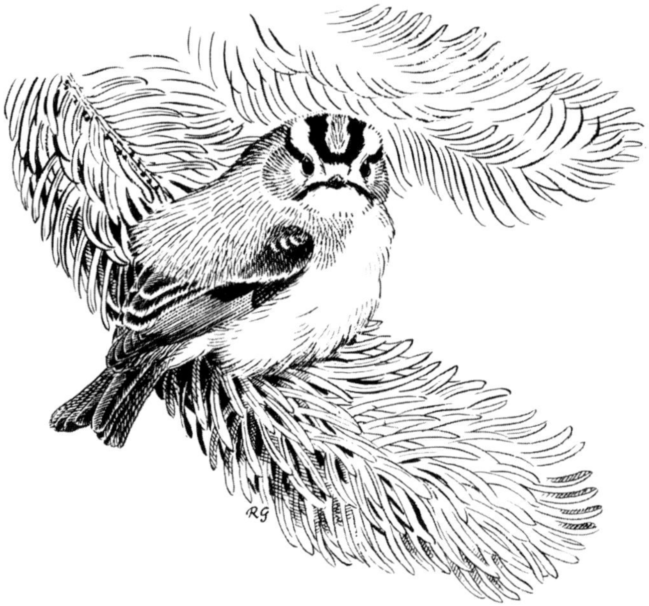

From 1974 the whole report was printed, and the sized reduced to A5, the traditional size and shape for so many publications. It is a size that naturally comes out of the large sheets of paper on which many pages are printed at the same time. When the sheets are folded and cut, the pages all tidily come together to form a section. They were still stapled but now through the middle and not the side. The first two of the new Reports were printed by Penna Press, run by my late brother. He had started Penna in his bedroom at our house in Northcourt Avenue, around 1953, after falling in love with printing at school. A new hobby group had been launched after the arrival of an old treadle printing press, the gift of a grateful parent. Harry Stevens had also taken to the craft with enthusiasm and the Printing Group soon settled into a room above the Headmaster's office. This group printed my first Christmas

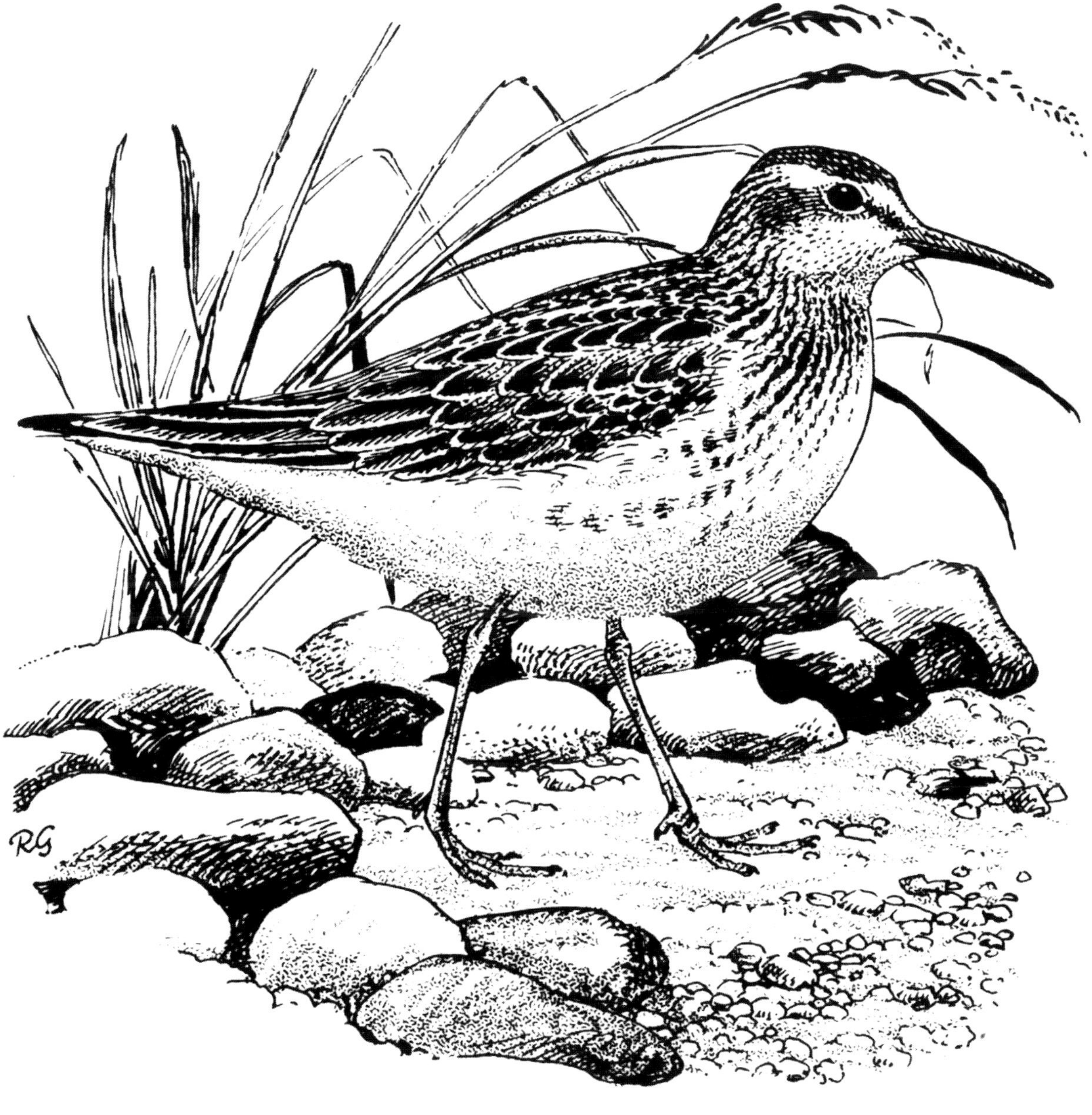
RG

cards for both the school and the ROC. Harry, as we have already seen, went on to print the ROC Report covers, and Penna Press saw to the printing of many of the later ROC Christmas cards and other ephemera.

Those early all-printed Reports were in black only throughout. Colour was not seen again for twelve years. The 1974 Report saw another significant change. It was now titled *The Birds of Berkshire* as it no longer seemed sensible to confine the Report to the restricted area around Reading that had made sense when it all started twenty-eight years earlier.

Looking back on these artworks I can assess them as if they were the work of another hand and consider them critically. For instance I do not think that the Firecrest on the first printed Report is one of the better ones! I cannot now recall why it was chosen and it looks as though perhaps I was not so involved as in some. Perhaps my marriage to Sue in October 1974 and our trip to East Africa in the following spring took my mind temporarily away from the work in hand!

At this time publication was beginning to slip. For years it had been possible to publish a year's records during the following year, but the Report for 1974 was not out until 1976 and 1975 was also published two years later. In order to catch up, the first double issue, combining the Reports for 1976 and 1977, was published in 1978.

A real rarity and another first for Berkshire, a Sharp-tailed Sandpiper from east Siberia, turned up at Reading Sewage farm in August. It featured on the 1975 cover, and Avocets appear for the second time on the double issue. By now I had seen and sketched Avocets in the field and the difference between these and the bird I had drawn in 1951 is striking. But then, so it jolly well should be!

Sprint Print in Basingstoke had now taken on the printing and the next three drawings, all on coquille board, are not particularly noteworthy. But in 1977, the Report for 1975 broke new ground with line

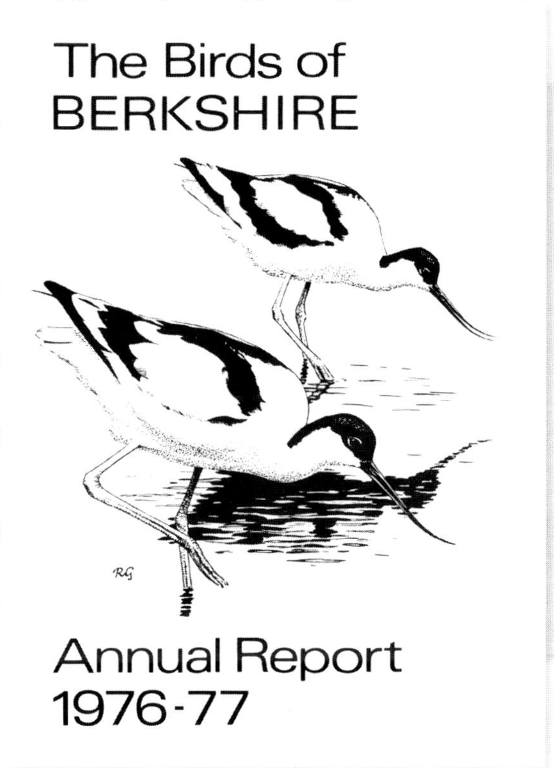

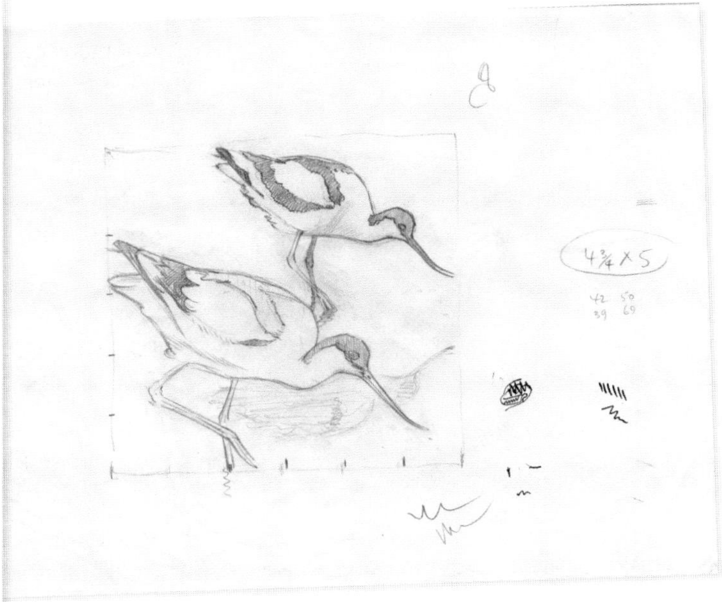

The Birds of Berkshire 1976–77. Avocets, line drawing on coquille board

illustrations inside for the first time. These were by a young Reading artist, Norman Arlott, having a first chance to see his work in print. He illustrated the next five Reports and in 1981 won the *British Birds* Bird Illustrator of the Year Award. He has gone on to a long and distinguished career as one of the country's leading bird illustrators. In 1985 another young Reading artist, Martin Hallam, took over providing text illustrations and is still supplying excellent drawings to this day. He was also to win the coveted *British Birds* Award in 1988.

The Birds of Berkshire 1978.
Brent Geese, line drawing
on coquille board

The Birds of Berkshire 1979.
Caspian Tern, line drawing
on coquille board

The Birds of Berkshire 1980.
Long-eared Owl, line drawing
on coquille board

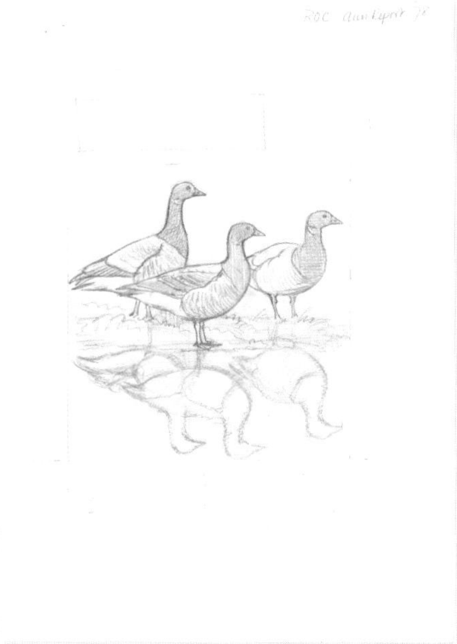

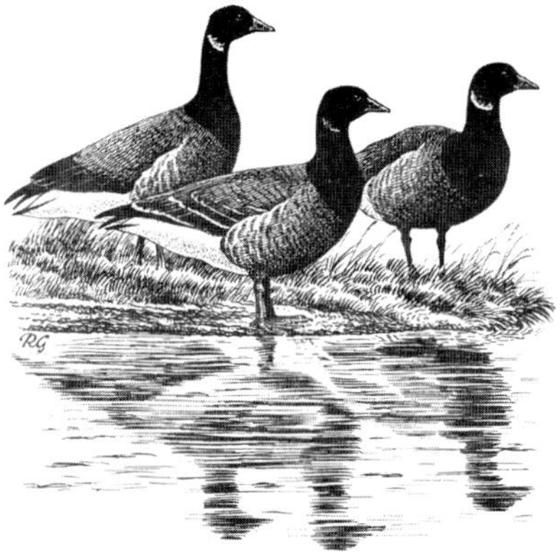

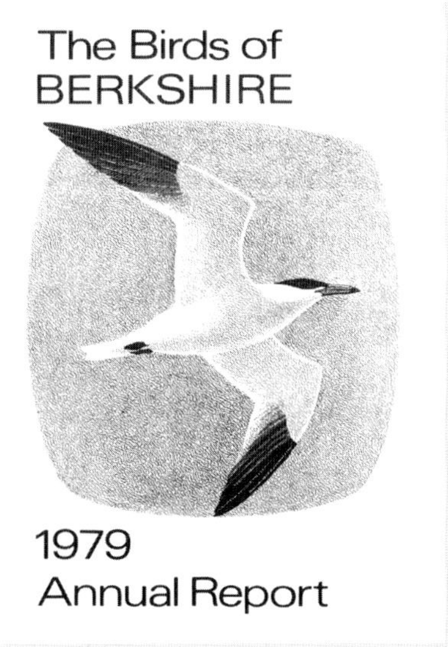

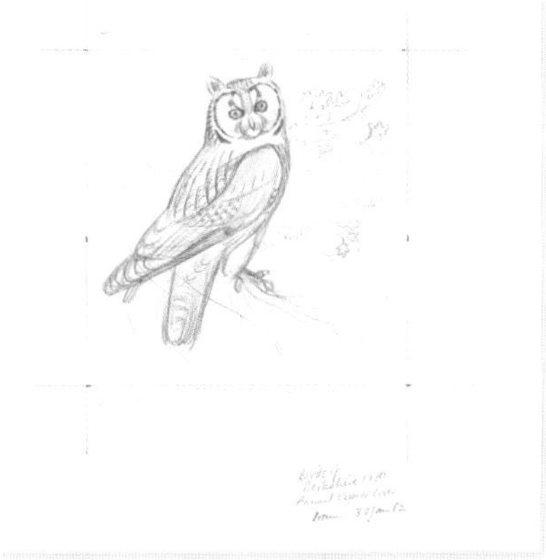

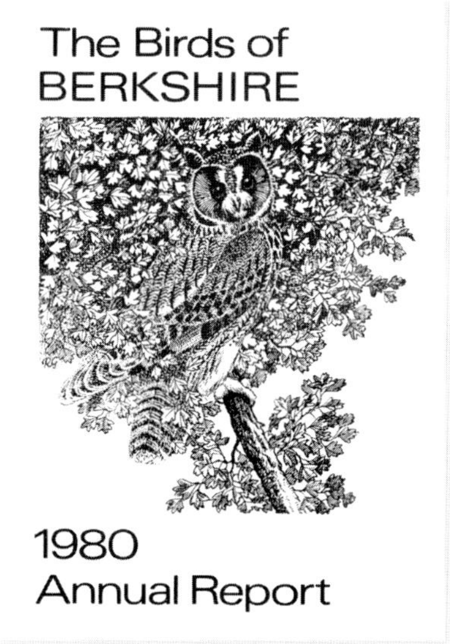

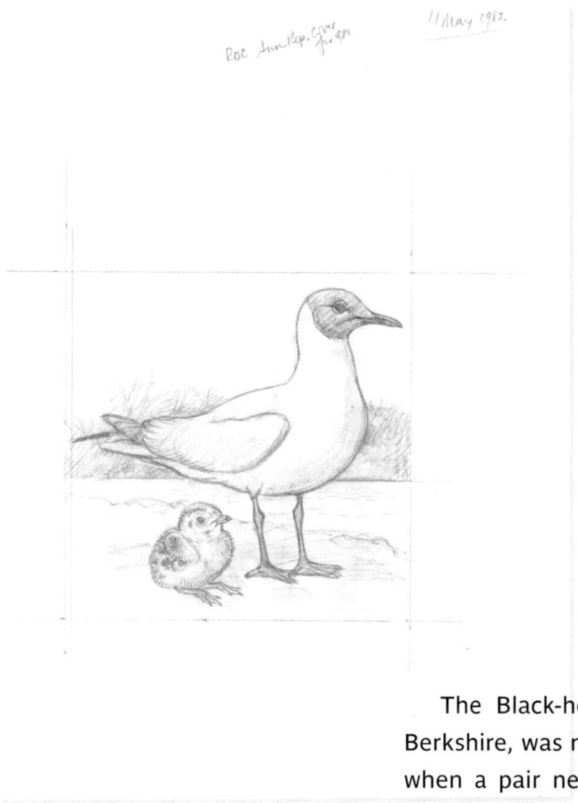

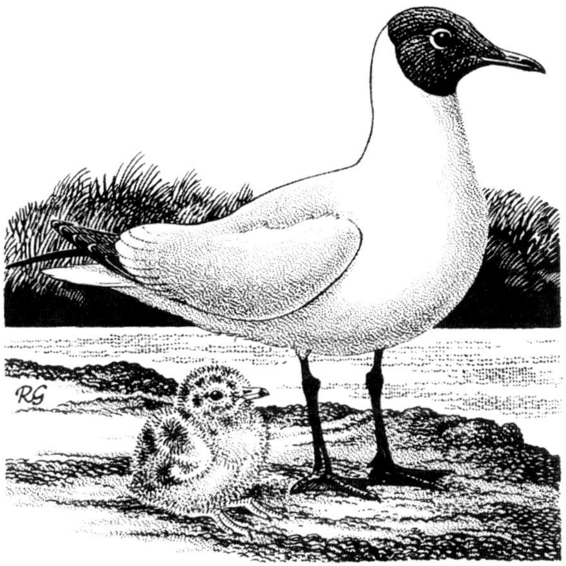

Sketch for 1981 report,
Black-headed Gull and chick

The Birds of Berkshire 1981.
Black-headed Gull and chick,
line on coquille board

The Black-headed Gull, although by far the commonest gull in Berkshire, was not recorded as breeding in the Reading area until 1981 when a pair nested at Theale Gravel Pit. Sadly, the single chick did not survive for more than a few days. The event was marked with that year's cover, published in 1983. Yet another rarity, a Scarlet Rosefinch, which had appeared in an Earley garden in May, adorned the double volume covering 1982/3 published eventually in 1985. Also known as the Common Rosefinch, it breeds to the east of Europe, into Asia, and winters in India. However, our bird occurred in the same year, 1982, when a pair surprisingly nested in Scotland. There are many reasons which can cause delays in publishing. There is an increasing amount of work involved in processing a growing quantity of data coming in from larger numbers of observers. Recorders are doing the work voluntarily and out of true love of the whole business of recording accurately the birdlife of

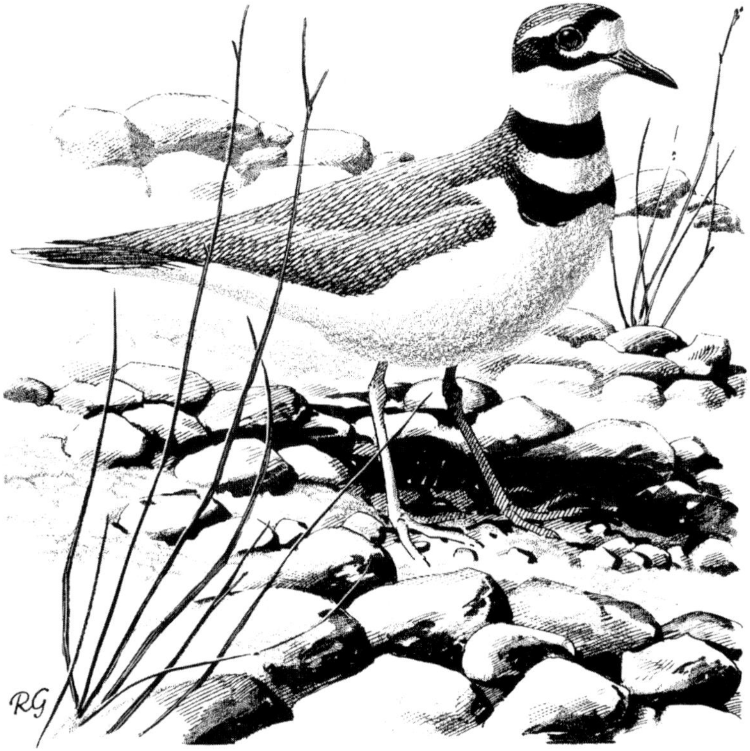

The Birds of Berkshire 1984.
Killdeer, line drawing on coquille board

Opposite page:
The Birds of Berkshire 1985.
American Wigeon, line drawing on scraperboard

their area. As people get older there may be new pressures on their lives which add to the burden of getting a Report out quickly.

In 1984 and 1985 two more American visitors excited local birders and became cover stars. The Killdeer Plover is an annual winter vagrant from North America and one spent eight days at Holyport Gravel Pit from 25 February. The American Wigeon is, like the Killdeer, an annual straggler to Britain and a party of four turned up at Thatcham Gravel Pit in November 1985.

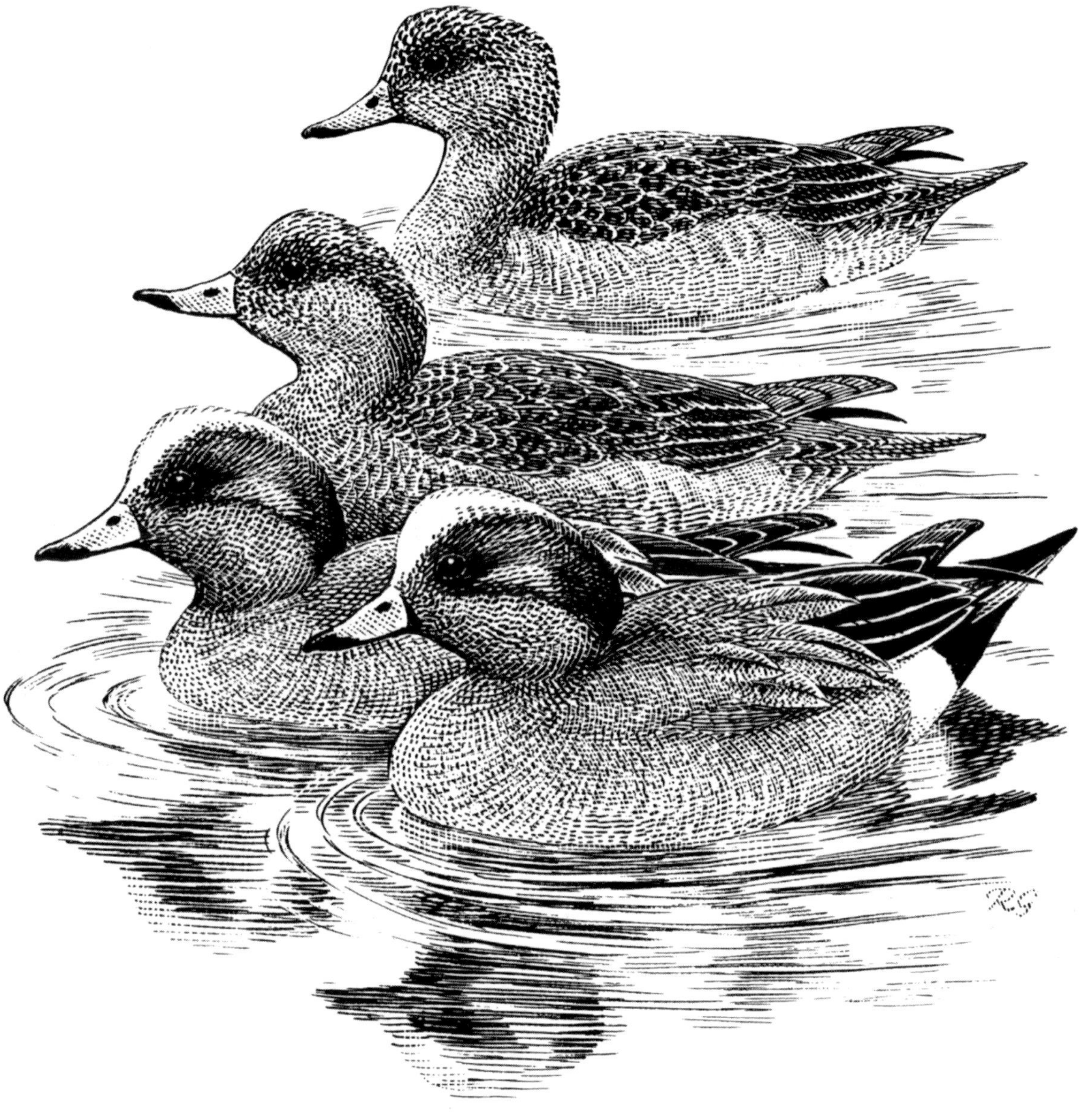

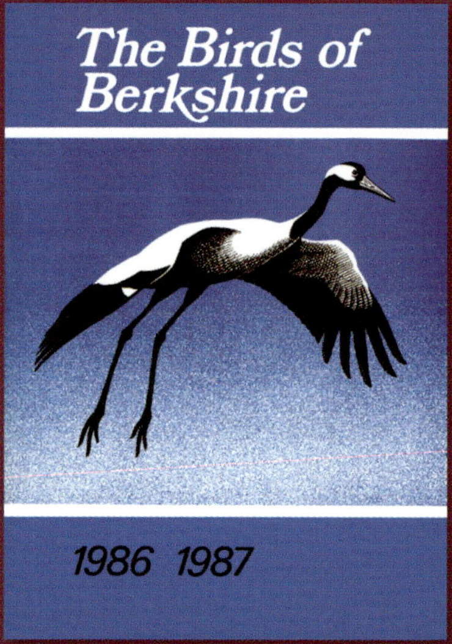
The Birds of Berkshire
1986 1987

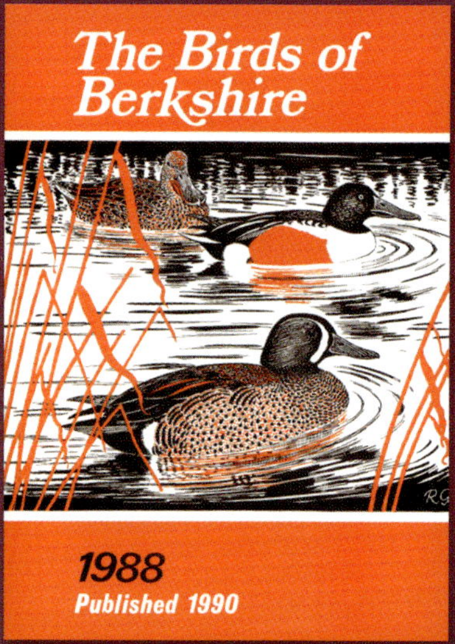
The Birds of Berkshire
1988
Published 1990

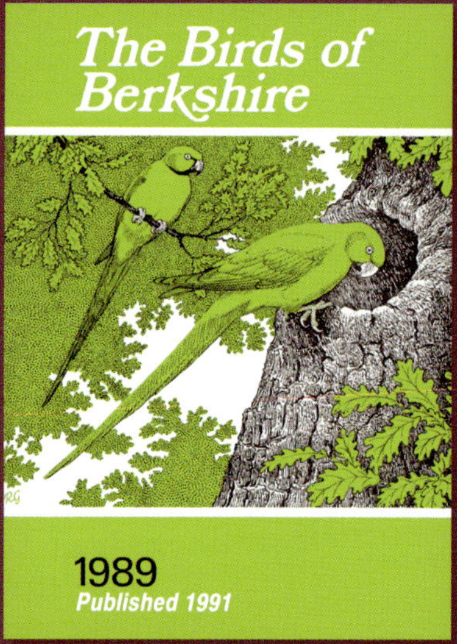
The Birds of Berkshire
1989
Published 1991

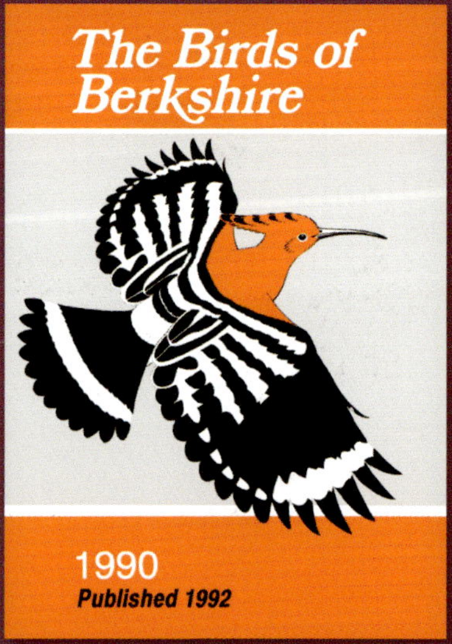
The Birds of Berkshire
1990
Published 1992

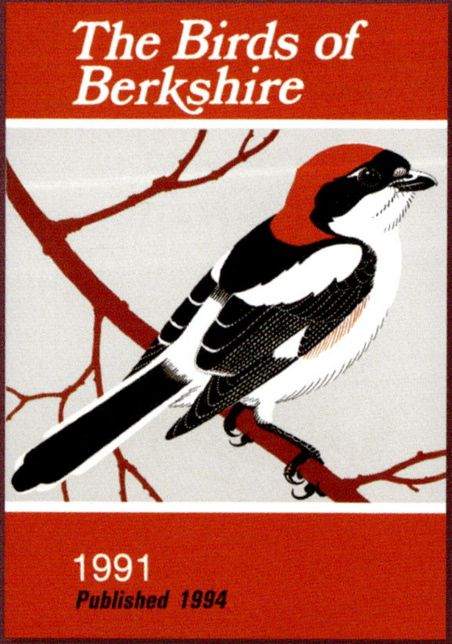
The Birds of Berkshire
1991
Published 1994

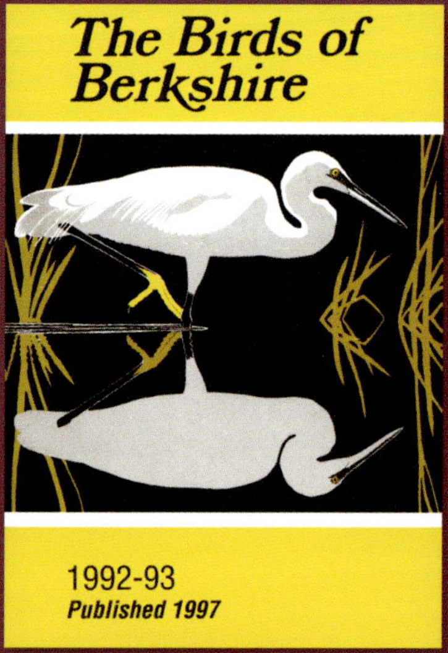
The Birds of Berkshire
1992-93
Published 1997

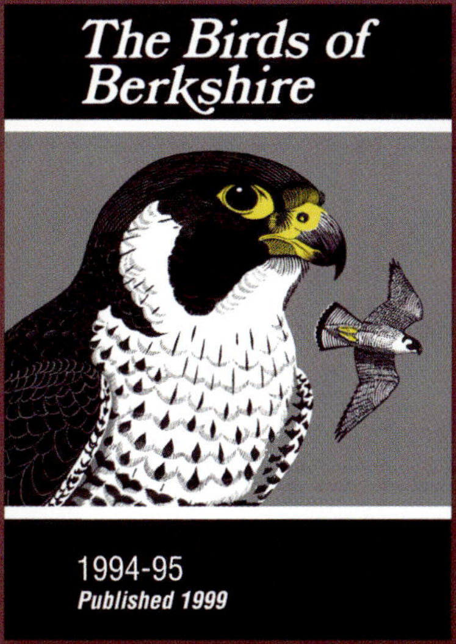
The Birds of Berkshire
1994-95
Published 1999

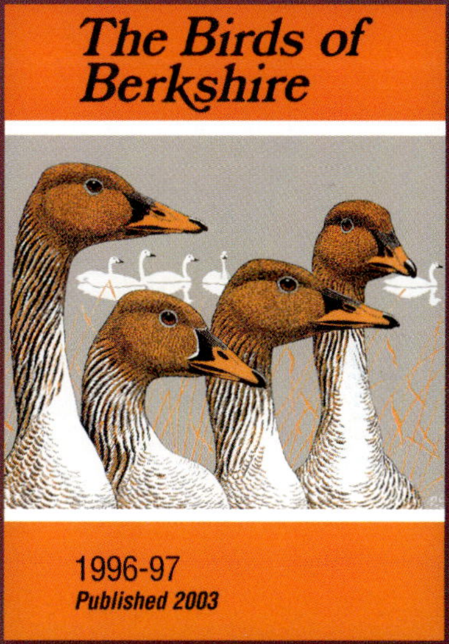
The Birds of Berkshire
1996-97
Published 2003

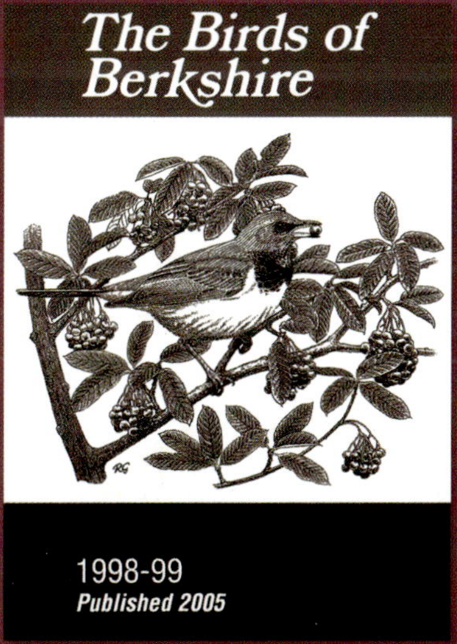
The Birds of Berkshire
1998-99
Published 2005

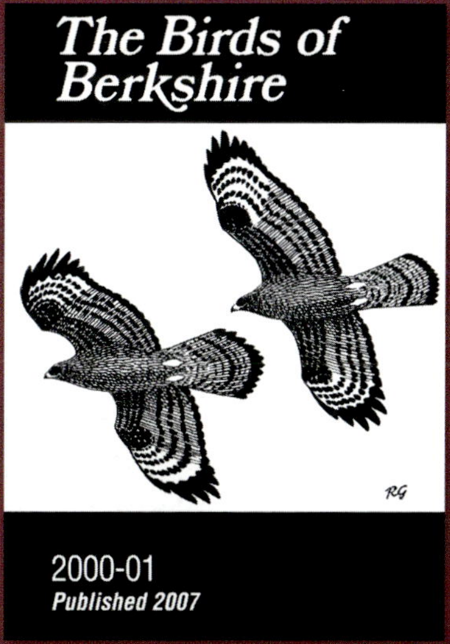
The Birds of Berkshire
2000-01
Published 2007

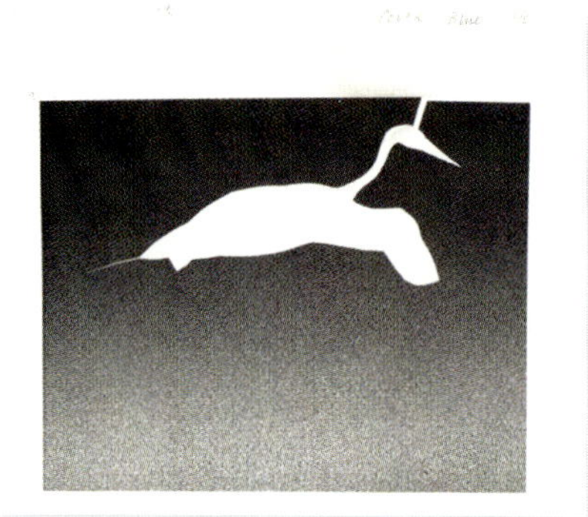

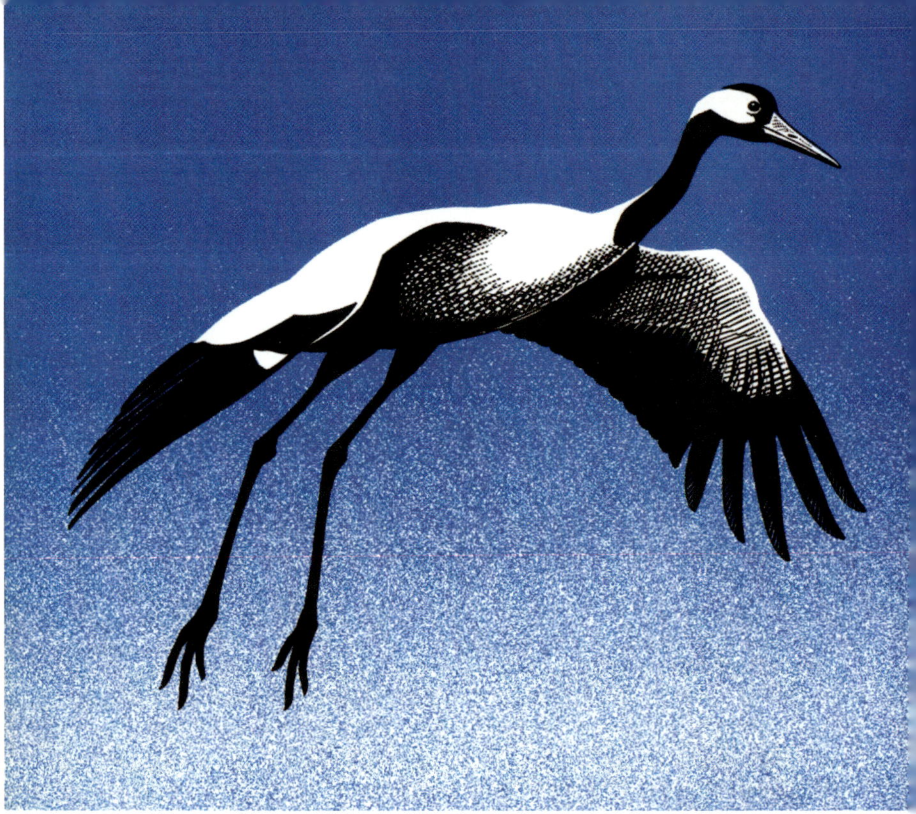

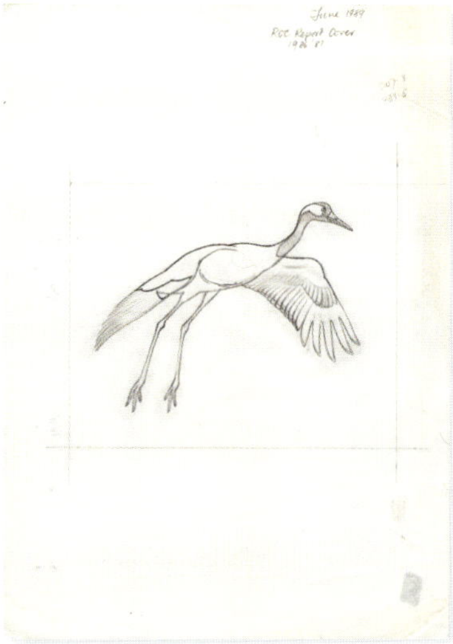

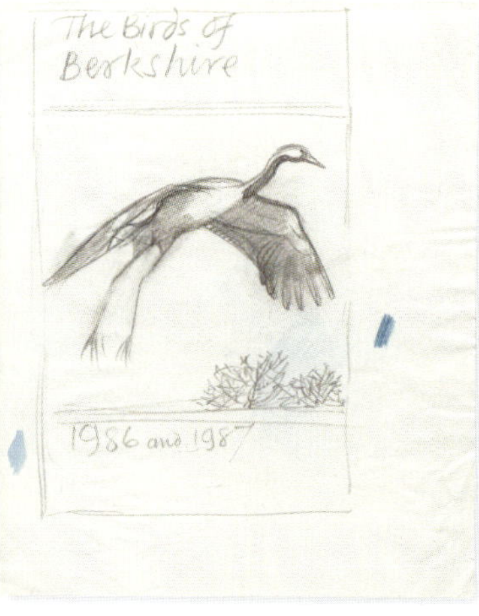
The Birds of
Berkshire
1986 and 1987

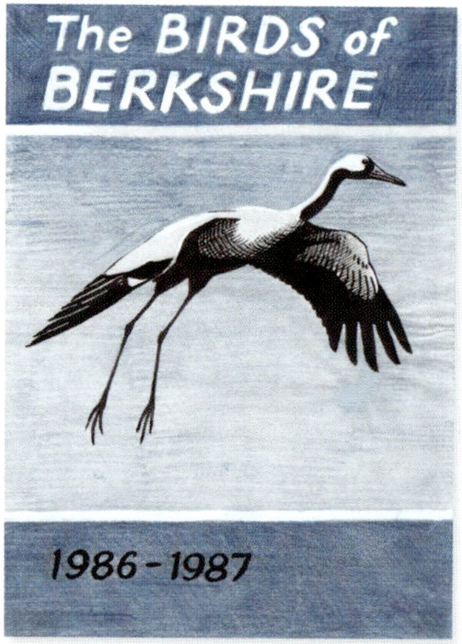
The BIRDS of
BERKSHIRE
1986 - 1987

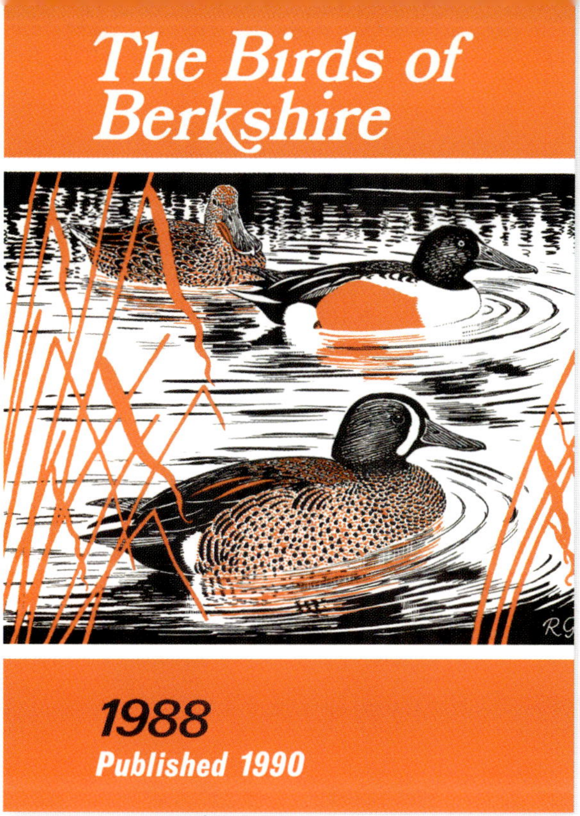

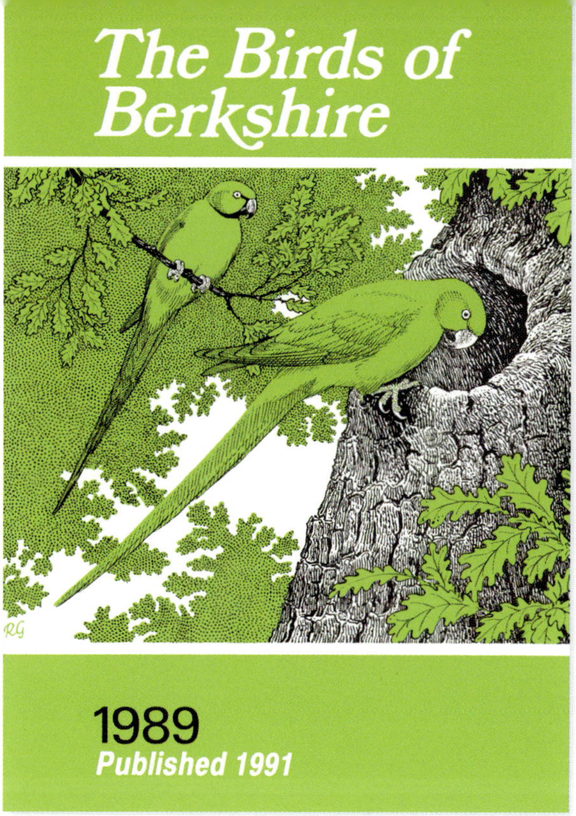

Opposite page:
The Birds of Berkshire 1986–7.
Crane, line drawing on scraperboard.
Mechanical tint and cover illustration

The Birds of Berkshire 1988.
Blue-winged Teal, line drawing
on scraperboard

The Birds of Berkshire 1989.
Ring-necked Parakeets, line drawing
on scraperboard

1986 and 1987 were published together in 1989, with the first of new two-colour covers with fresh typography. The drawing is of a Crane, wings and legs lowered for landing. The second colour, strong blue, is used on the panels at the top and bottom, carrying the title and publishing details. The artwork was also using a different technique which I had been playing with in other work: the use of a mechanical tint, in this case a tint of the blue. Tints came in the form of black printed, self-adhesive, rub-down sheets and, for this design, I used a graduated tint that goes from dark to light in tone. It was cut out to fit around the scraperboard drawing of the Crane itself. I made use of different tints on future covers as they can give the impression of extra colours when only two have actually been used.

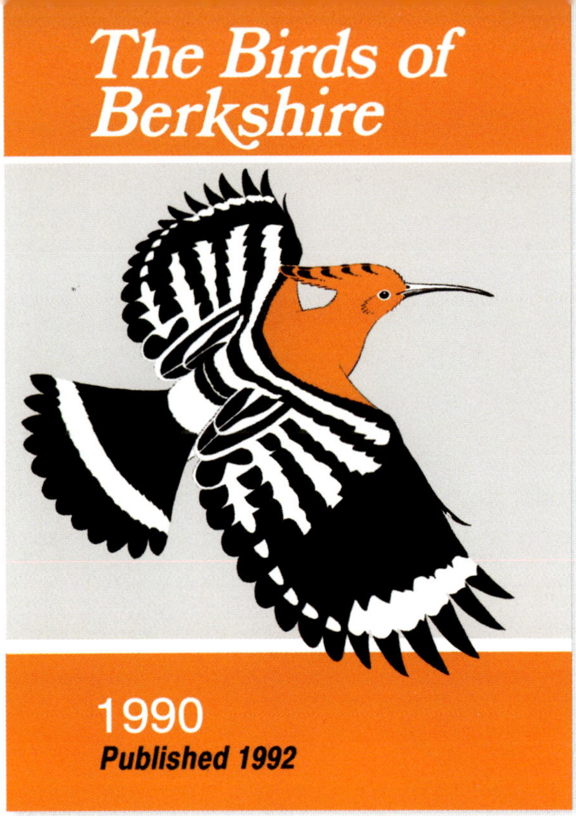

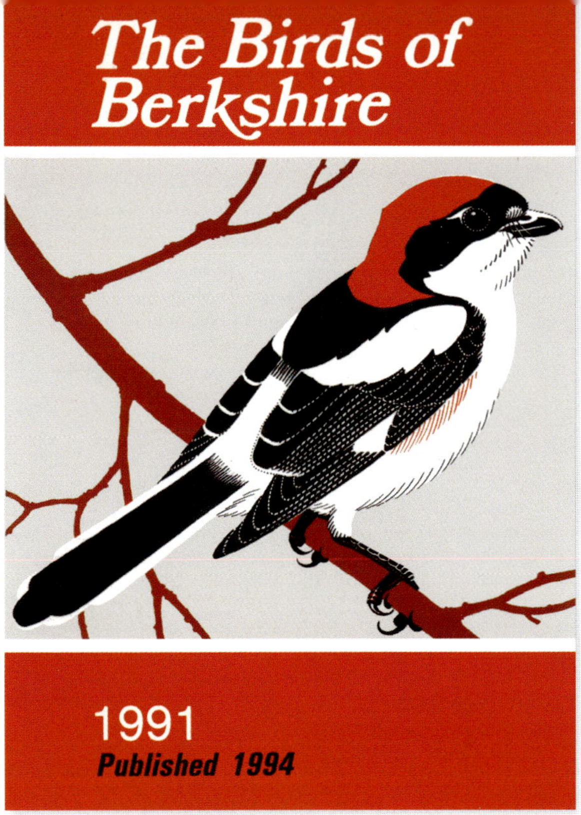

The Birds of Berkshire 1990. Hoopoe, two-colour line and tint

The Birds of Berkshire 1991. Woodchat Shrike, two-colour line and tint

The Birds of Berkshire 1992–3. Little Egret, two-colour line and tint

The Blue-winged Teal and Ring-necked Parakeets were also in two colours, but the extra colour was drawn in black on a transparent plastic sheet laid over the drawing of the birds to achieve precise registration.

The next three designs, taking the Reports from 1990 to 1992/3 (published 1997) all used tints of the black to give a grey background or, in the case of the Little Egret, to print with the yellow to make a greenish colour for the reeds. So in effect, the two colours printed on white, which counts as a colour, can produce black, grey (tint), yellow, green and white. Little Egrets have been the subject of much interest since their spectacular increase and spread around southern Britain from the fifties onwards. It is somewhat surprising that there was no record in Berkshire before 1991.

The Birds of Berkshire

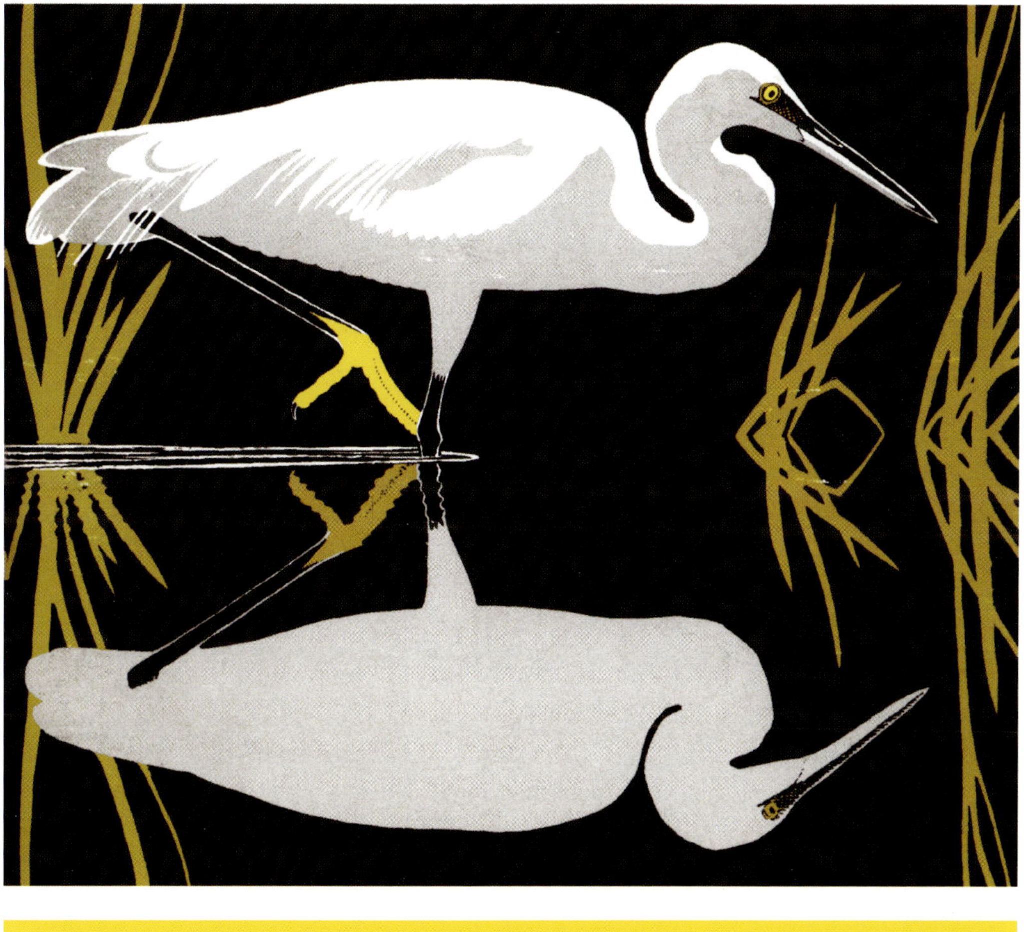

1992-93

Published 1997

The Birds of Berkshire

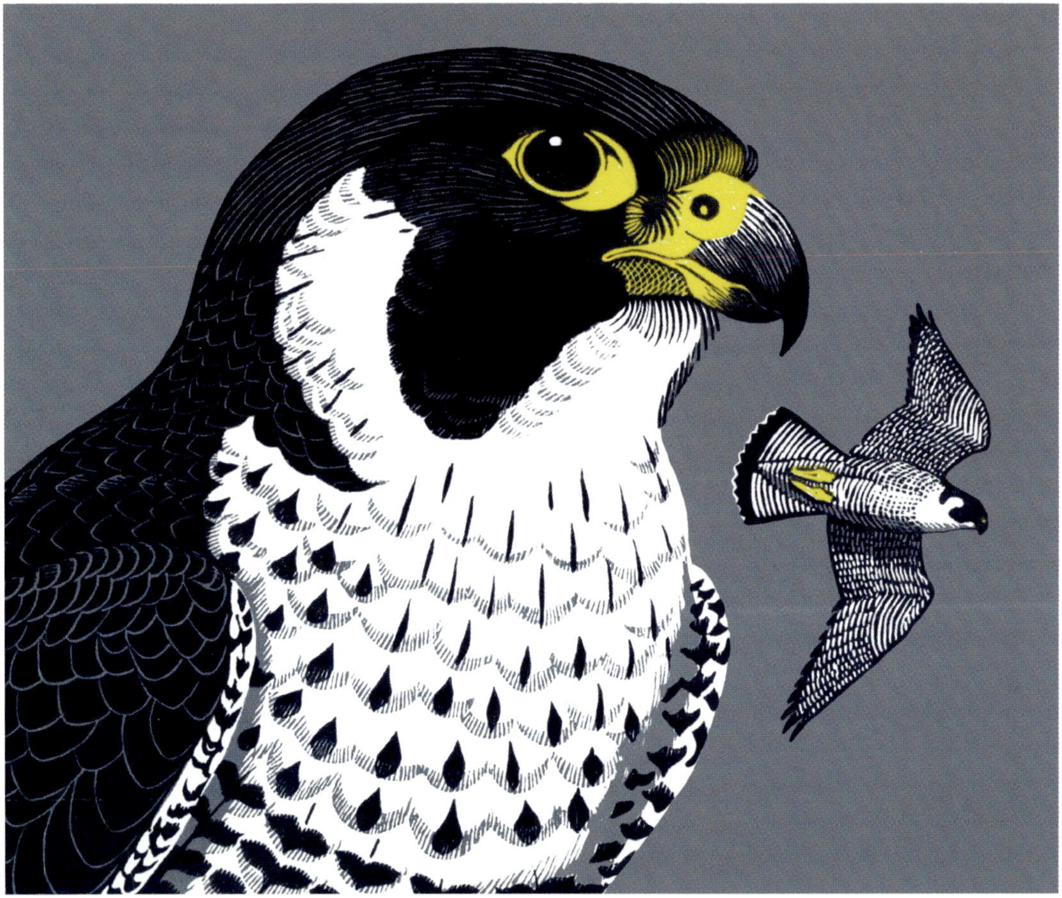

1994-95

Published 1999

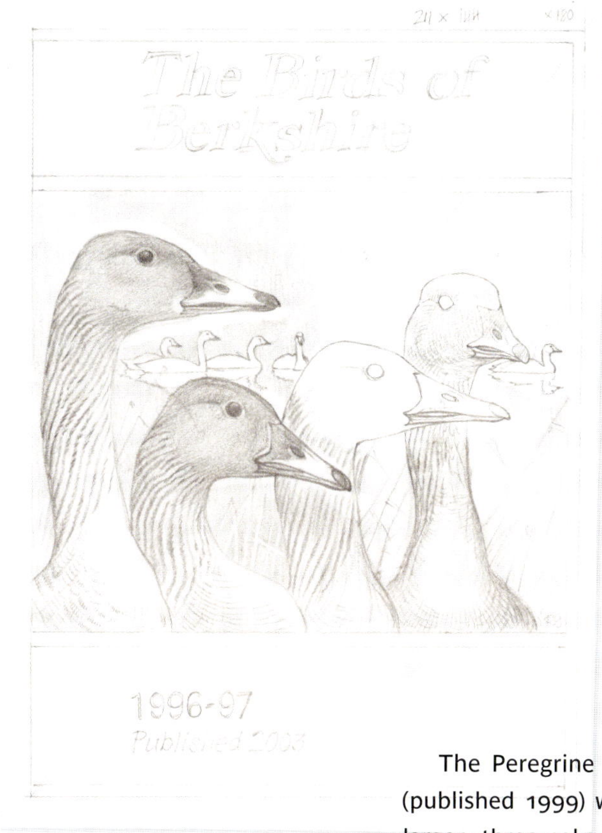

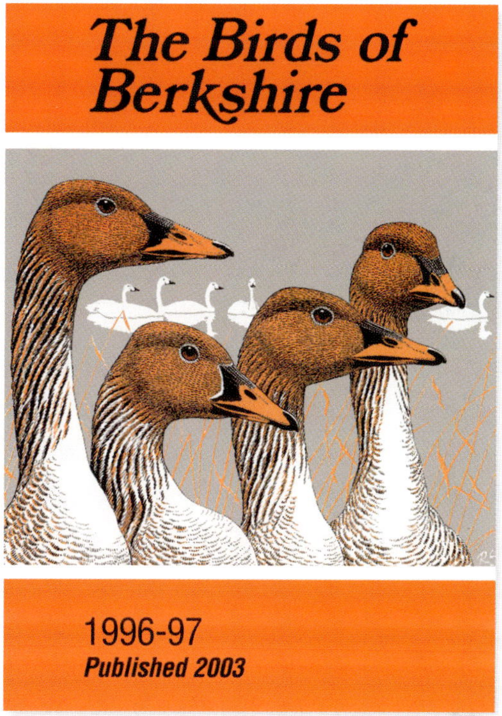

Opposite page:
The Birds of Berkshire 1994–5.
Peregrine, three-colour linocut

The Birds of Berkshire 1996–7.
Bean Geese, two-colour line and tint

The Peregrine Falcon on the cover of the double 1994/95 report (published 1999) was different again in that the original was a much larger, three-colour linocut print. It was not originally designed as a Report cover, but it seemed suitable so instead of black I suggested a very dark slatey blue, with a fine tint to make the light blue grey background. The second colour was yellow for the beak, eye and feet. The following Report, covering 1996/97, shows a group of Bean Geese which dropped in at Wigmore Lane in January 1997. This was another line drawing on scraperboard printed in black and orange with a tint of the black for a grey background, showing up a party of Bewick's Swans.

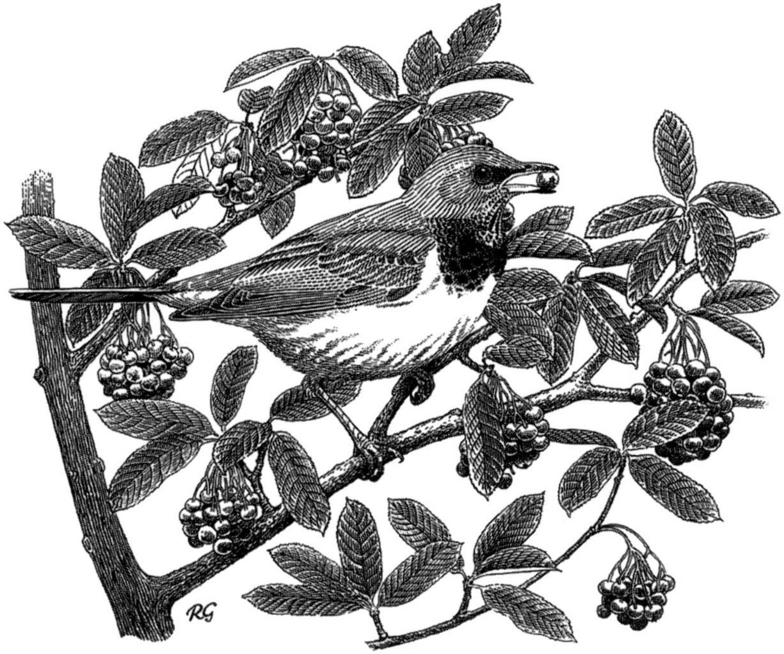

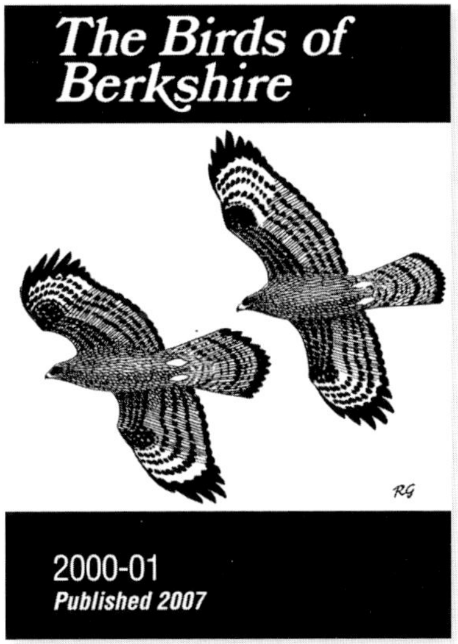

The Birds of Berkshire 1998–9. Black-throated Thrush, line on scraperboard

The Birds of Berkshire 2000–01. Honey Buzzards, line drawing

The double Report for 1998/99 highlighted the first record for Berkshire of a very rare vagrant, a Black-throated Thrush, a handsome immigrant from Siberia. Odd birds find themselves straying off course into western Europe, usually in late autumn or winter. This was printed in black with a dark tint for the panels framing the drawing.

The following cover of Honey Buzzards (2000/01) was also printed in one colour – black, with no tints. This was the longest Report to date with 172 pages, so perhaps the cover was deliberately cost conscious?

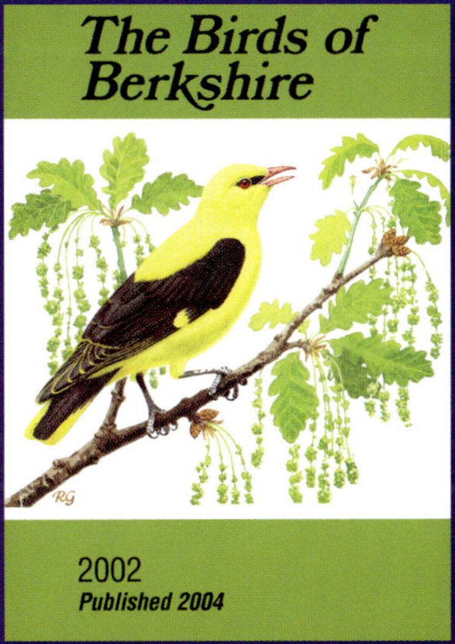
The Birds of Berkshire
2002
Published 2004

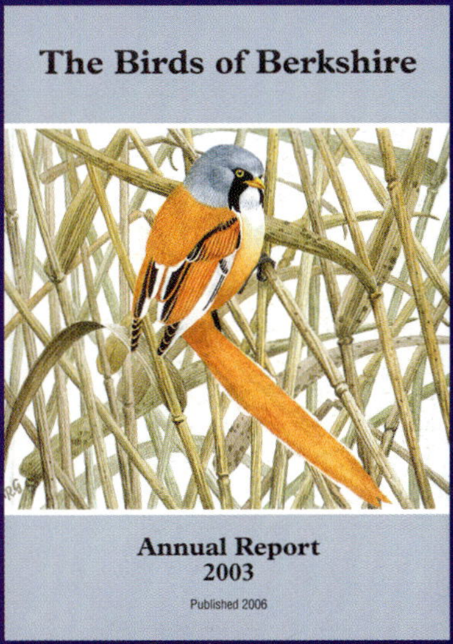
The Birds of Berkshire
Annual Report
2003
Published 2006

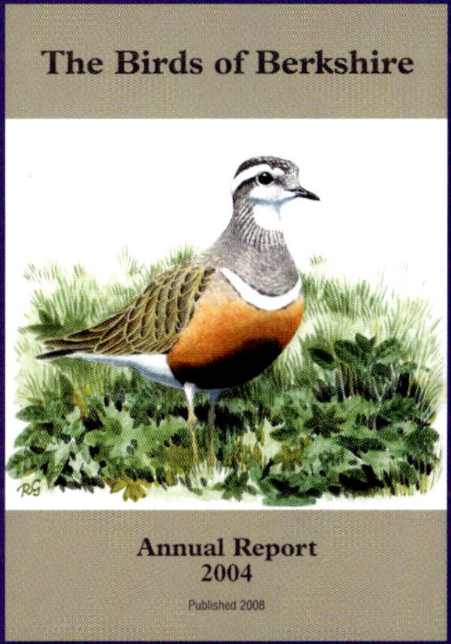
The Birds of Berkshire
Annual Report
2004
Published 2008

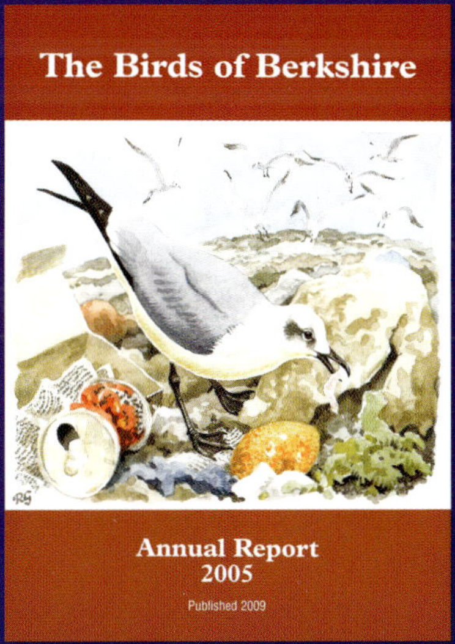
The Birds of Berkshire
Annual Report
2005
Published 2009

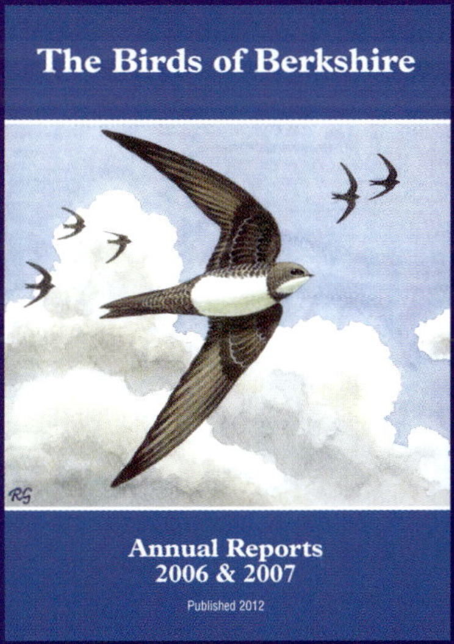
The Birds of Berkshire
Annual Reports
2006 & 2007
Published 2012

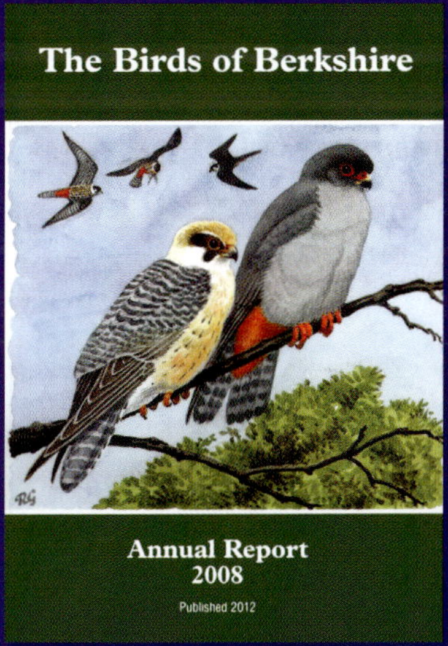
The Birds of Berkshire
Annual Report
2008
Published 2012

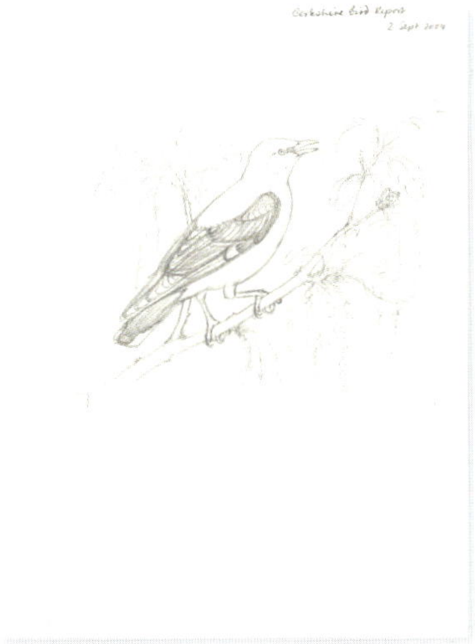

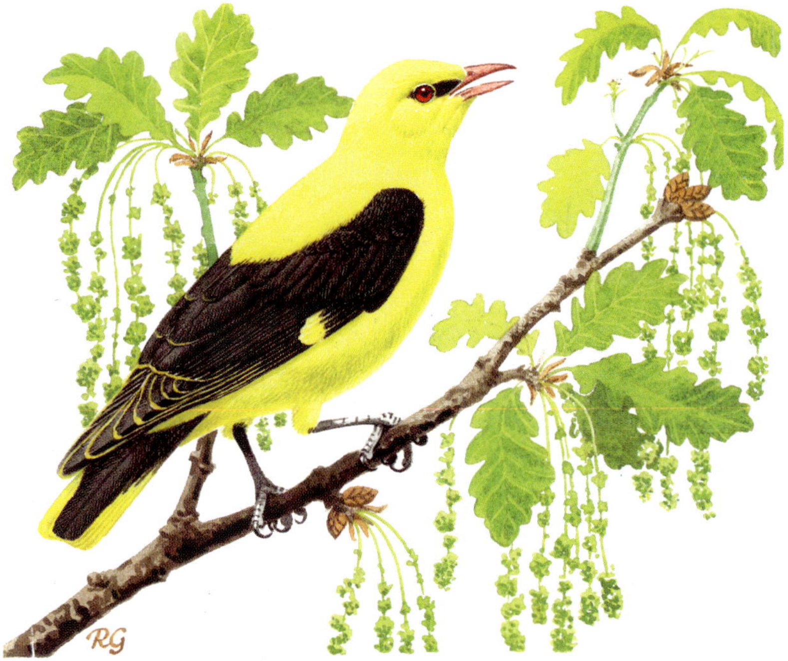

The Birds of Berkshire 2002.
Golden Oriole, watercolour

Opposite page:
The Birds of Berkshire 2003.
Bearded Tit, watercolour

However the Report for 2002 revealed the next, and perhaps most exciting, new departure – the first full colour cover, reproducing a watercolour painting of that most colourful bird the Golden Oriole. Not a particularly rare bird but surprisingly difficult to observe despite its bright colours, as they blend with sun-dappled leaves in the canopy. It is a summer visitor and there is a small breeding population in the East Anglian fens. So colour had arrived at last and from then on there was no going back, and all the covers since then have been in full colour. Nowadays these are practically the only watercolour paintings I do as I have given myself over almost entirely to printmaking.

The Reports had included black and white photographs since the first printed Report for 1974. At first they suffered from pretty inadequate

The Birds of Berkshire

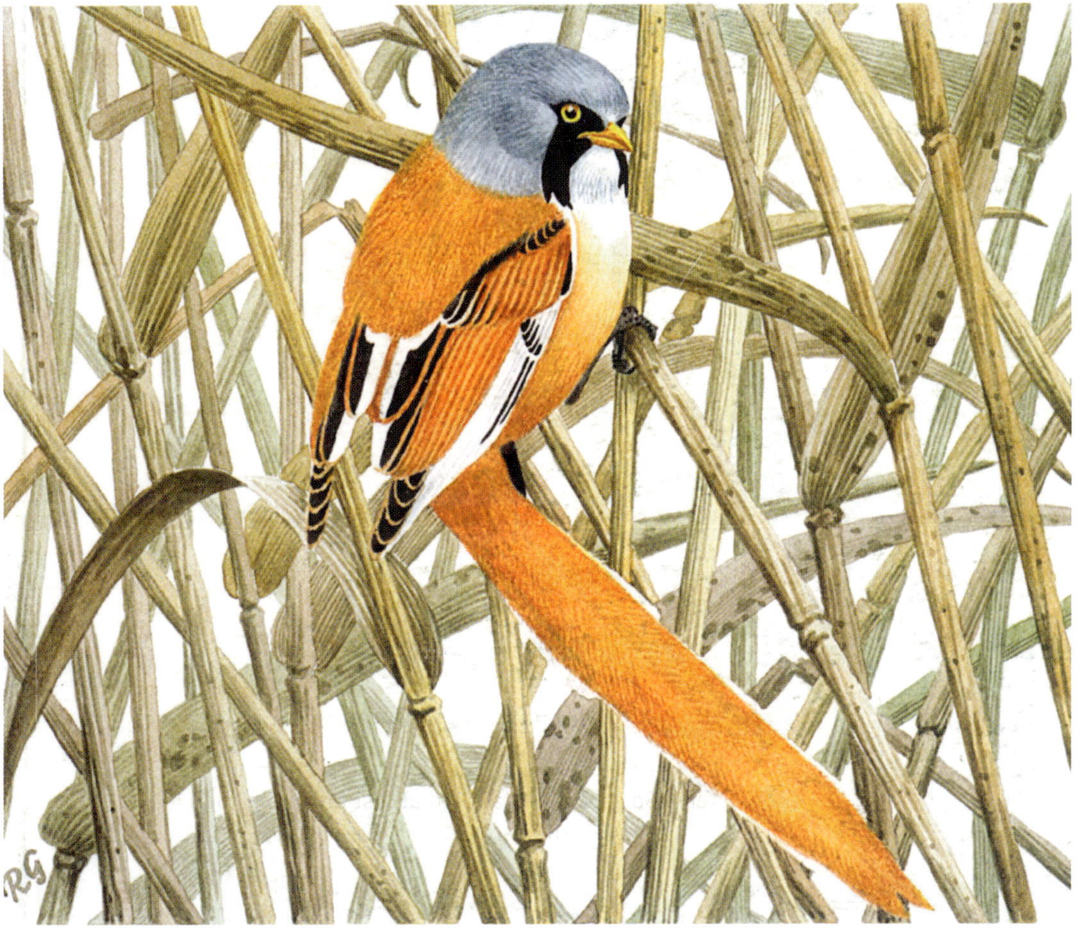

Annual Report
2003

Published 2006

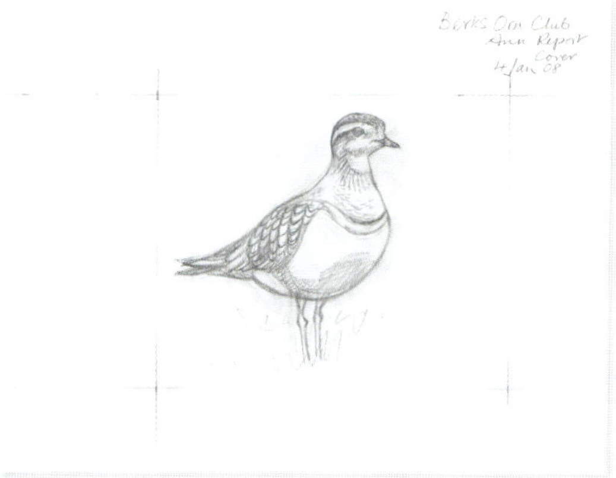

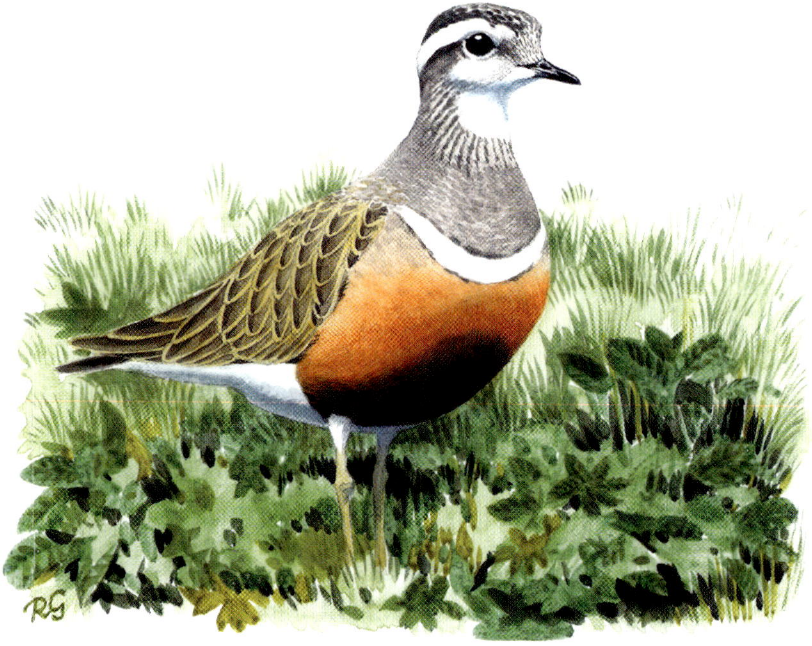

The Birds of Berkshire 2004.
Dotterel, watercolour

reproduction, improving as the cover card and paper stock improved. But with the advent of colour it is now possible to print colour photographs of a high quality by some of the Club's talented photographers. They had been enormously encouraged by the ROC President, the late Gordon Langsbury FRPS, widely acknowledged as one of the country's leading wildlife photographers.

The Peregrine cover was my first since we moved from Reading to Norfolk in 1998. The 2003 cover showed the influence of the move, with a cock Bearded Tit among reeds, just as I could see them almost any day I cared to walk down the lane onto the Reserve. The Berkshire bird was seen at Burghfield Mill Gravel Pit at the end of the year. This Report also had a change of typography and surprisingly, for the first time, the words 'Annual Report' preceding the year.

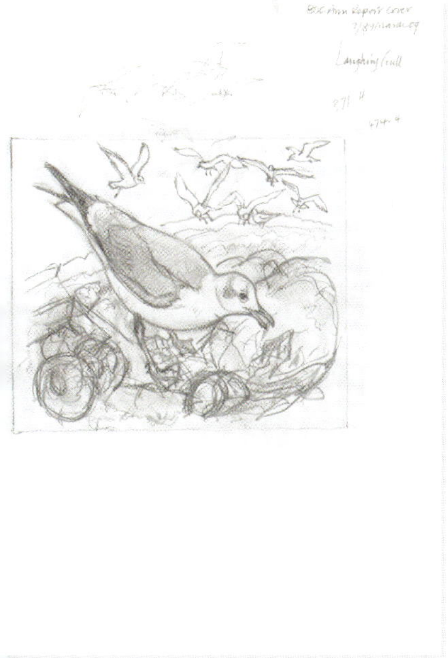

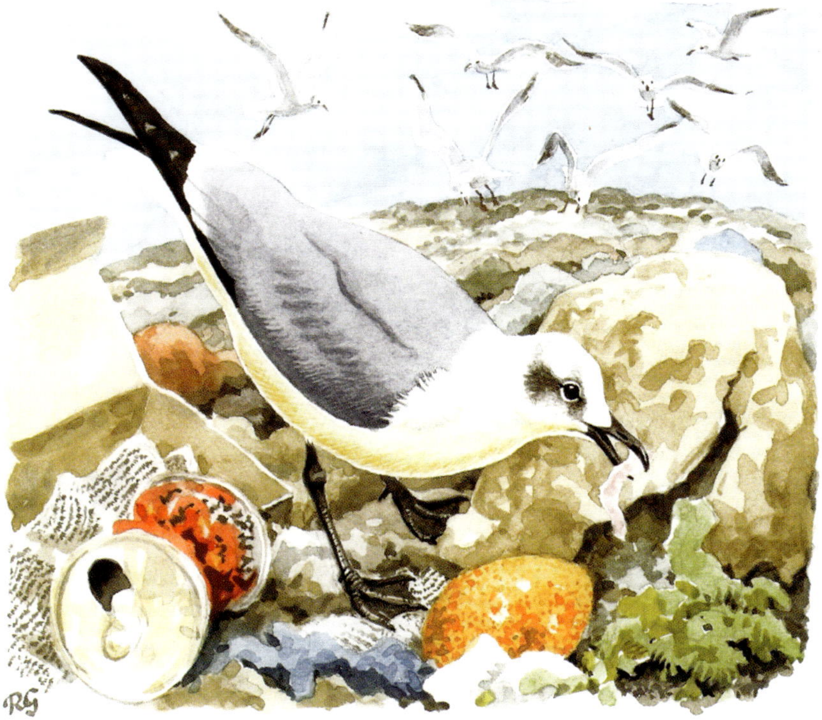

The Birds of Berkshire 2005.
Laughing Gull, watercolour

A Dotterel, seen at Bury Down on 17 May 2004, was the subject of the next watercolour. As with the phalaropes, Dotterel females are much brighter than the males. This bird, with its duller plumage, was probably a male heading north where it would take a much greater part in the incubation of the eggs and care of the young. Nevertheless, a delightful bird with subtle colouring.

It was followed in 2005 (published 2009) by another Berkshire first. The setting for a Laughing Gull, a rare vagrant from North America, is less attractive as it joined the local gulls to feed on a waste tip. Its name derives from its flight-call, a strident 'Kee-agh'.

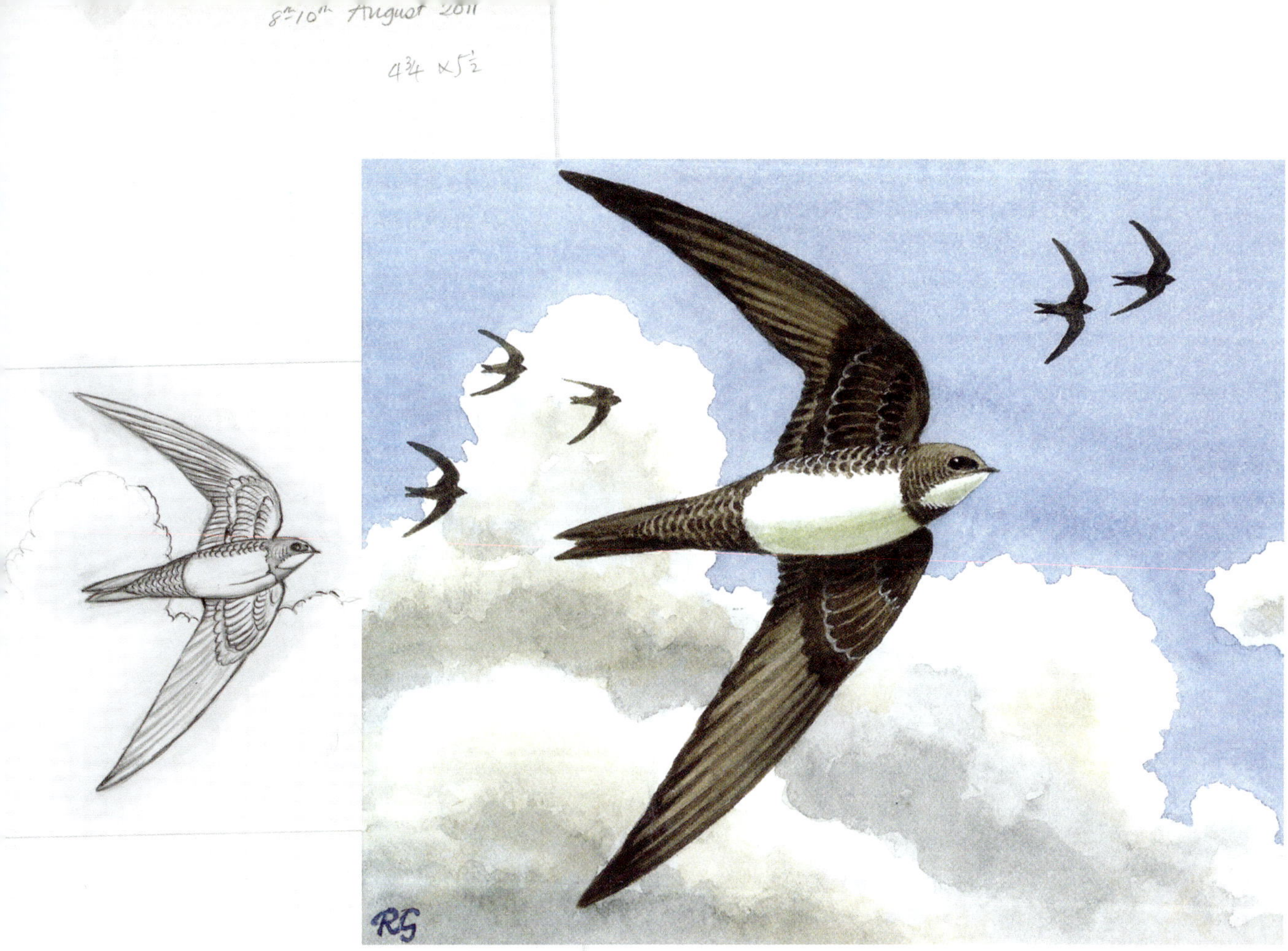

The Birds of Berkshire 2006–7.
Alpine Swift, watercolour

The painting for 2006/7 took to the skies again with an Alpine Swift, a larger cousin of our own, all dark Swift, some of which are circling in the background for comparison. There were two sightings in April during a national influx of this species in spring 2006. I had not realised when I did this painting that it was my fiftieth ROC Annual Report cover. The Club has been going for longer of course, but the doubling up of Reports means that the number of years and the number of Reports do

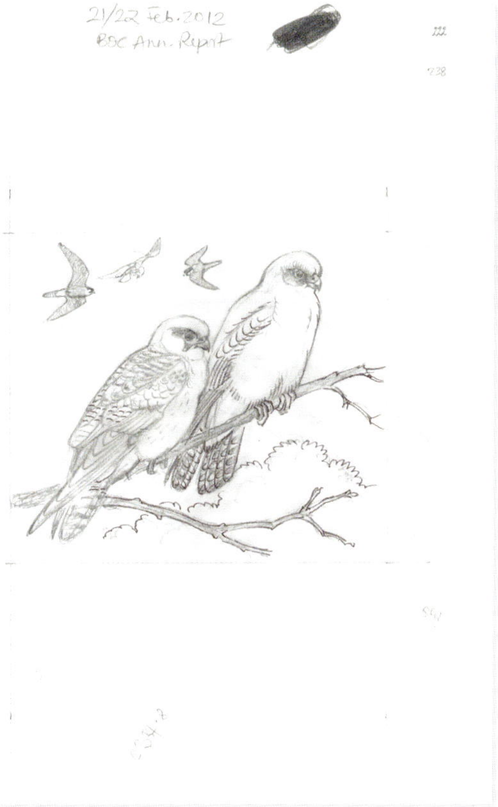

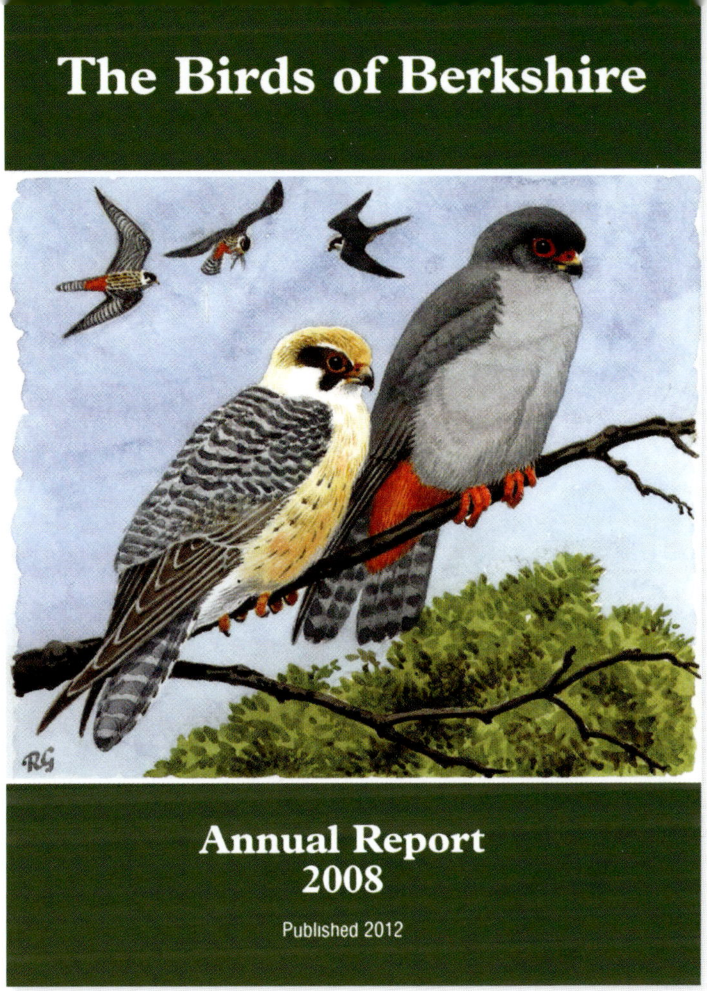

The Birds of Berkshire 2008.
Red-footed Falcons, watercolour

not coincide. And of course at the age of thirteen I hadn't thought that I would still be doing the same job over sixty years later!

In 2012 the Club published its Report for 2008 with the cover displaying a couple of Red-footed Falcons, colourful smaller falcons, not unlike the Hobbys in the distance. As with the Alpine Swifts, there was a spring influx of this delightful falcon into Britain, with over sixty reported, including the two in Berkshire.

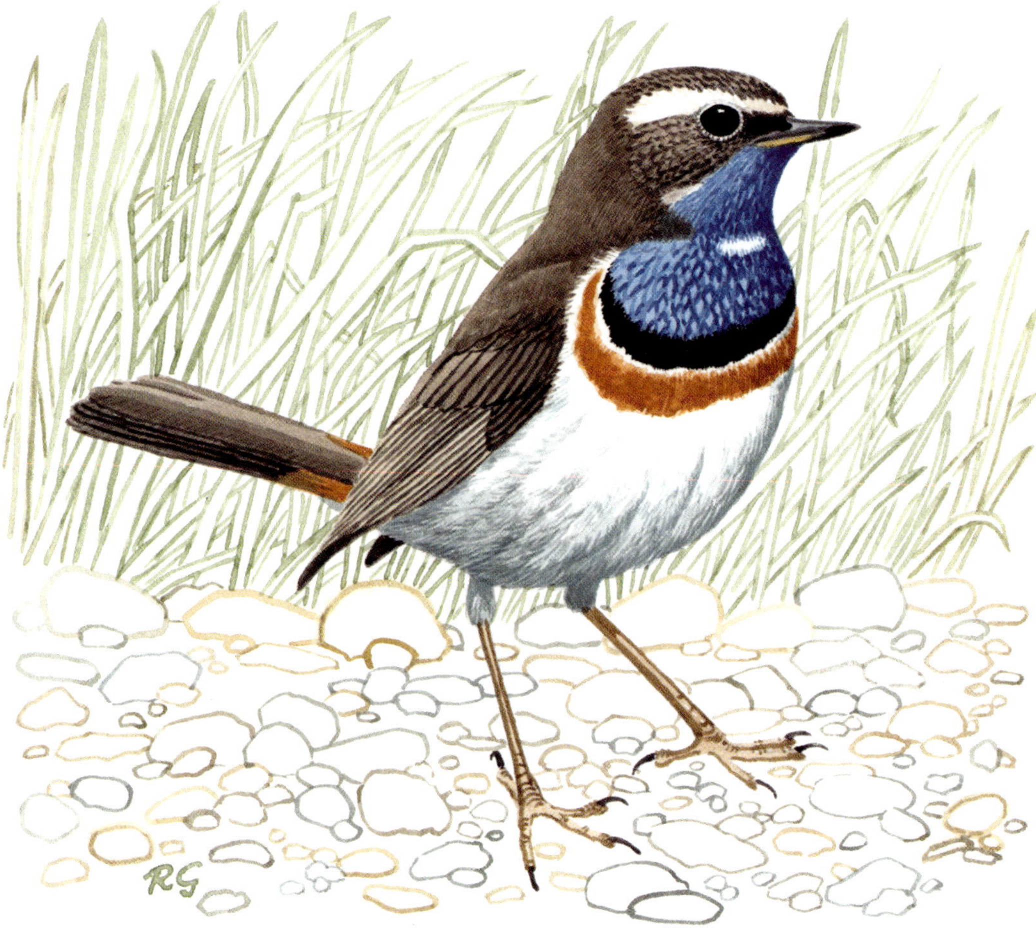

Watercolours for latest reports – Bluethroat and family of Oystercatchers

The latest reports continue to feature exciting ornithological records. A striking Bluethroat for 2009 and a family of Oystercatchers, marking the first recorded breeding in Berkshire of this large, mainly coastal wader in 2010. Bluethroats, Robin-sized birds, breed in northern Europe and overwinter from north-east Africa to west India. They are passage migrants to Britain in spring and autumn and are rare vagrants in Berkshire.

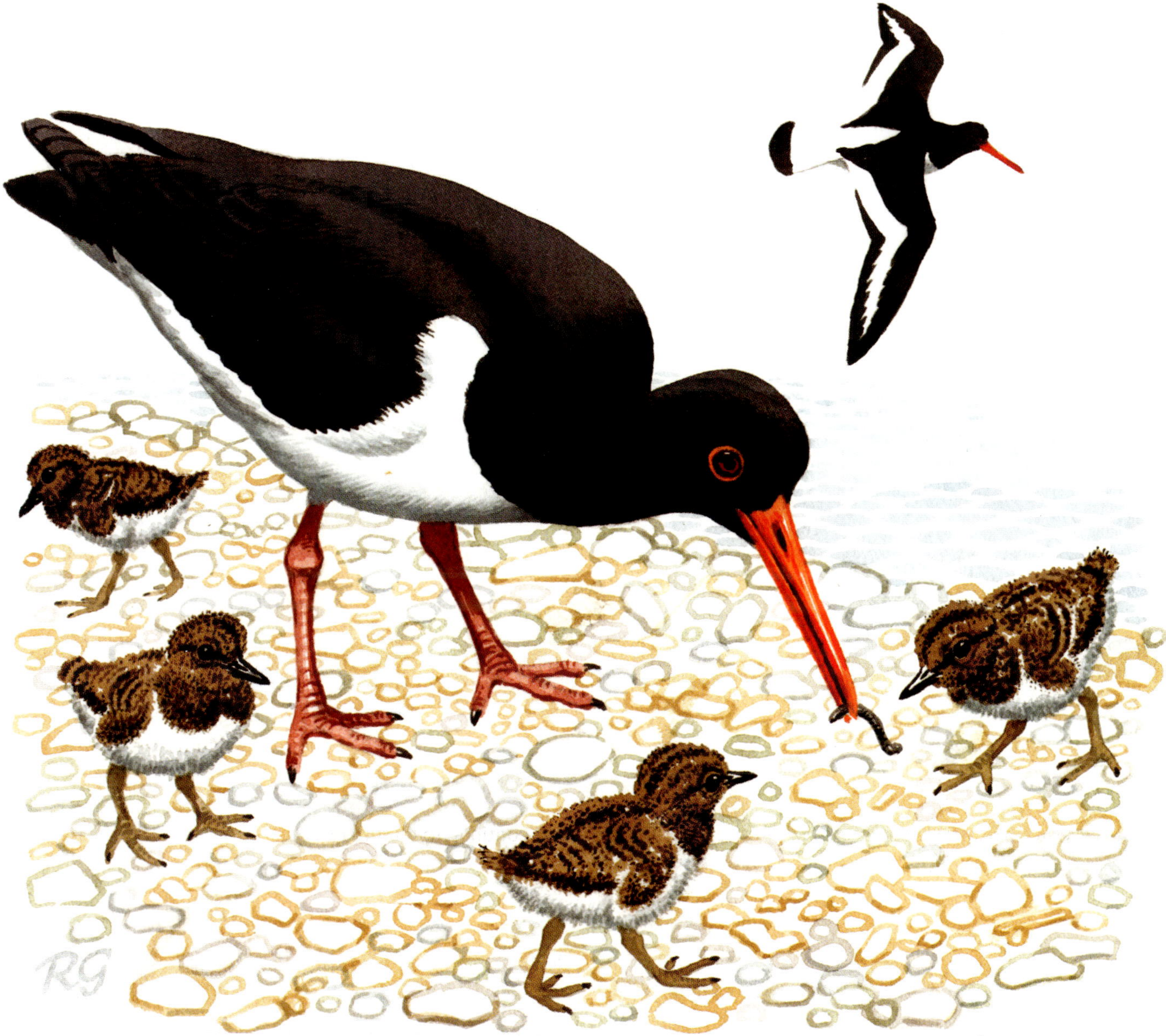
RG

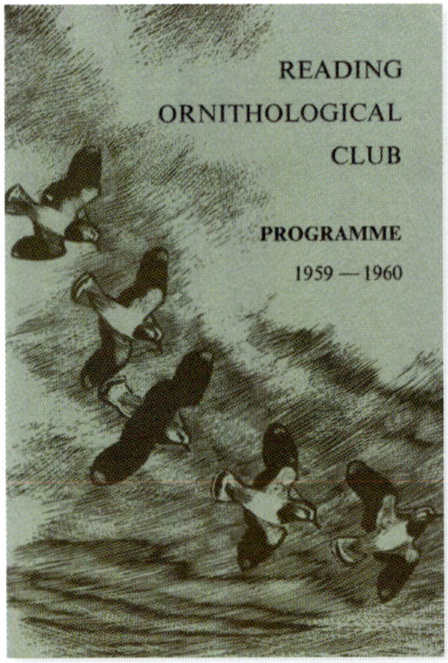

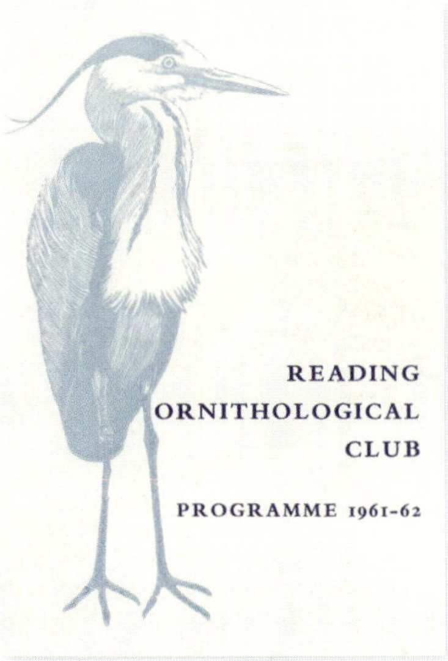

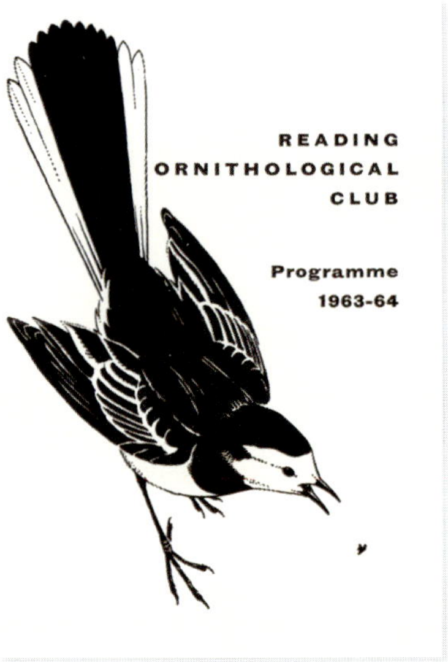

Programme cards 1959–60, 1961–62 and 1963–64

Opposite page:
Menu cards 1957 (10th anniversary), 1972 (25th anniversary), 1997 (50th anniversary) and 1987 (40th anniversary)

Over the years the ROC had used much other artwork, besides those covering the Club Reports. For at least nine years from 1958 I used to put an illustration on the small Programme card that heralded each winter season of meetings. These were a mix of line drawings and wood engravings, but no linocuts, presumably because of their small size. There were also promotion leaflets, menus for the six celebratory dinners when the Club reached an anniversary and, in the early days, Christmas cards. It was hoped that the latter would raise cash for the Club coffers, but I don't think they ever produced much. Among the ephemera were leaflets enticing new members with details of the attractions that membership would bring. The Tufted Duck was used in various forms until a simple design of a single drake became the official logo to appear on the Programme and newsletter, and any other official document.

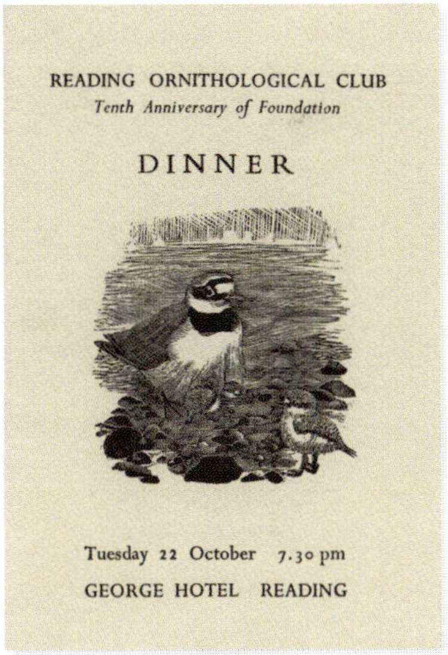
READING ORNITHOLOGICAL CLUB
Tenth Anniversary of Foundation
DINNER
Tuesday 22 October 7.30 pm
GEORGE HOTEL READING

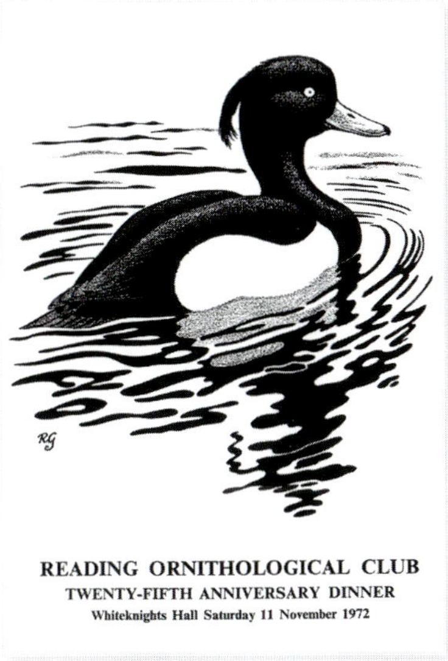
RG
READING ORNITHOLOGICAL CLUB
TWENTY-FIFTH ANNIVERSARY DINNER
Whiteknights Hall Saturday 11 November 1972

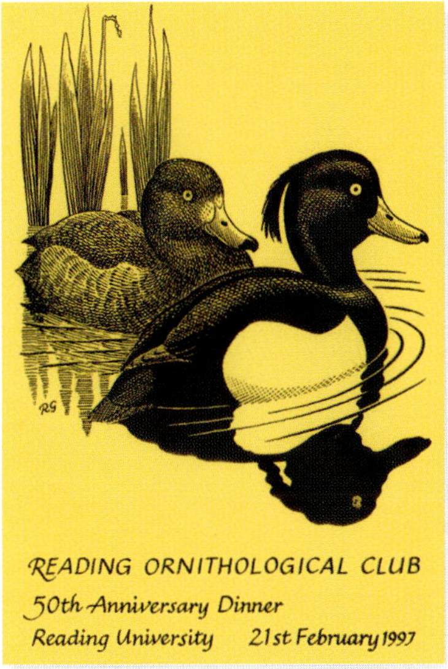
RG
READING ORNITHOLOGICAL CLUB
50th Anniversary Dinner
Reading University 21st February 1997

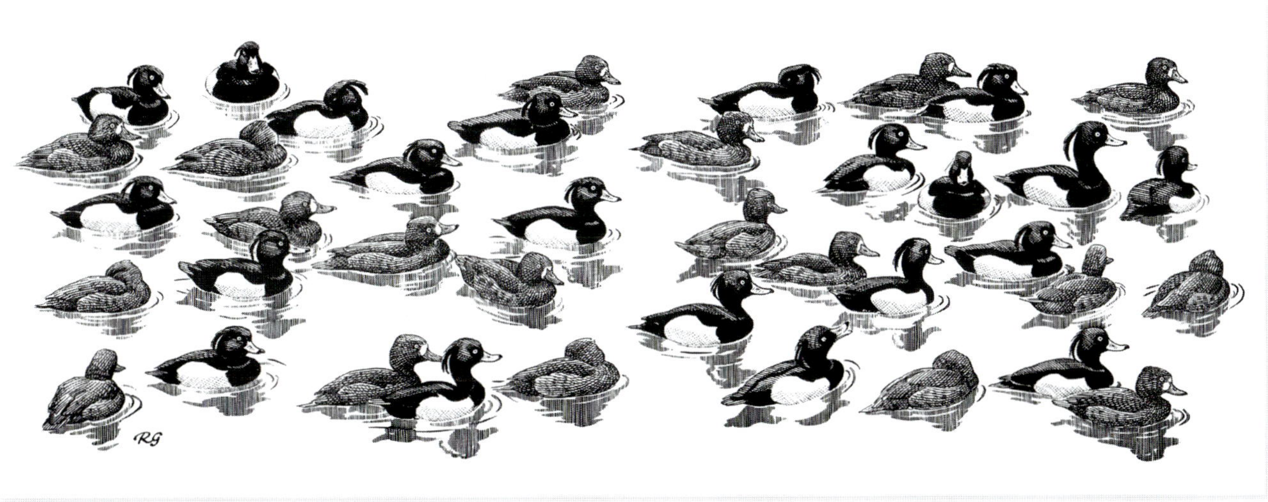
RG

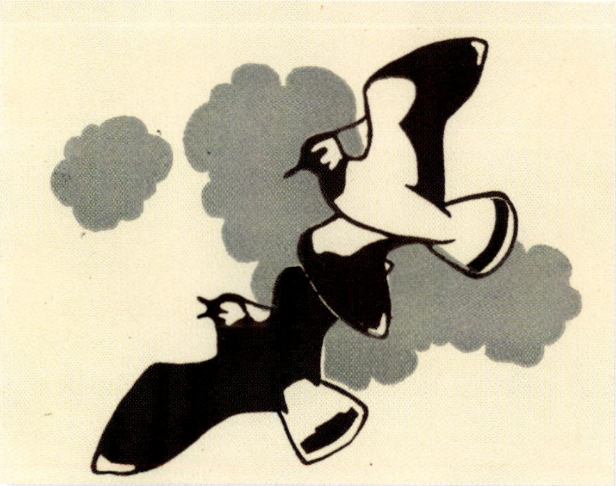

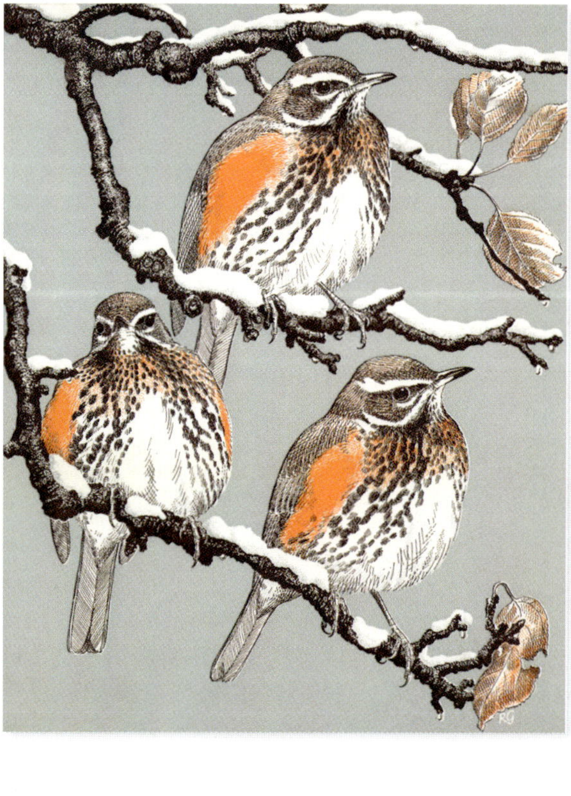

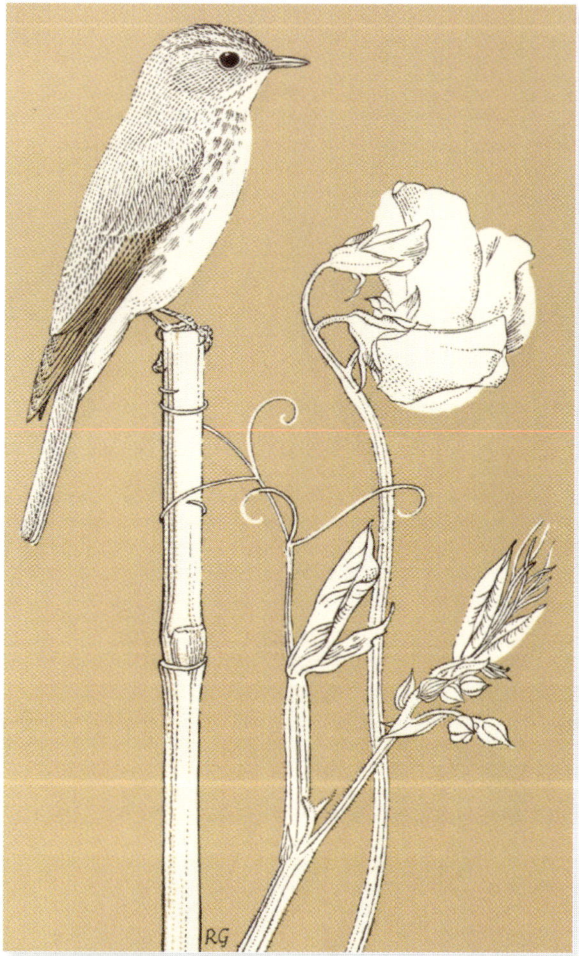

Christmas cards: 1952, Lapwings; 1965, Redwings; 1963, Spotted Flycatcher

Opposite page:
1964, Drake Smew; 1962, Bullfinch; 1956, Pintails; 1967, Wheatear

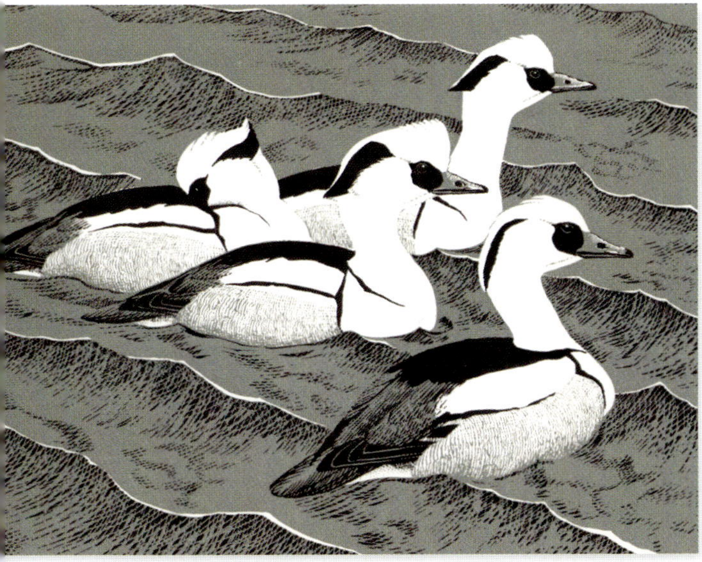

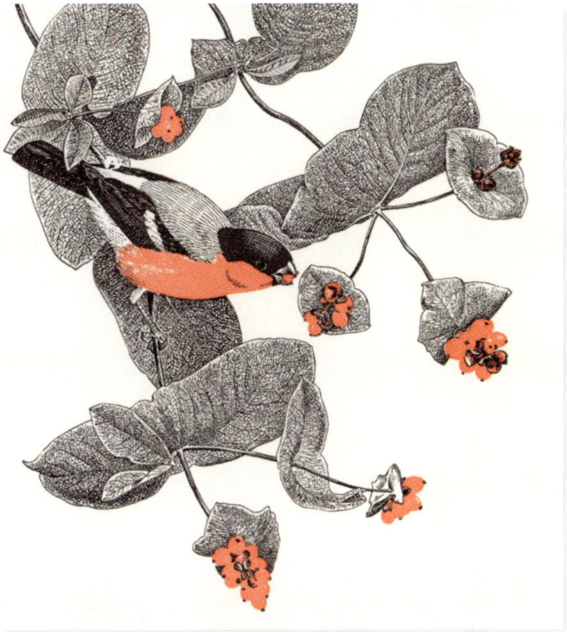

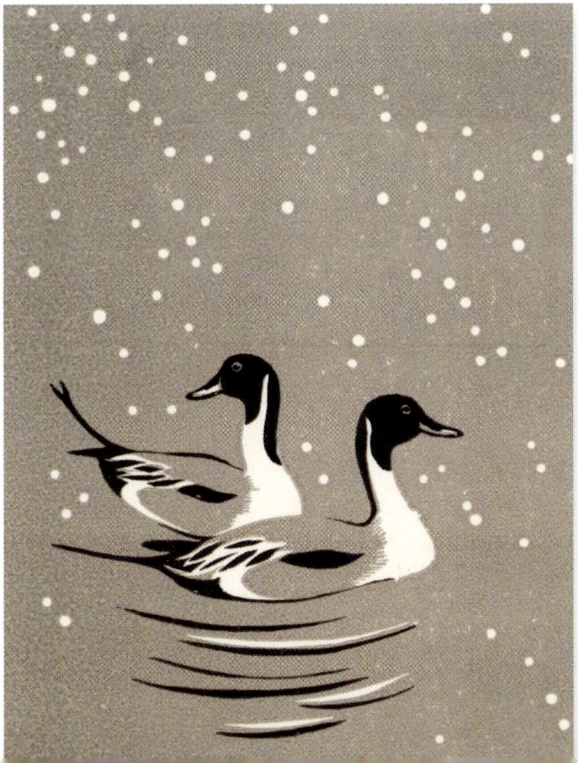

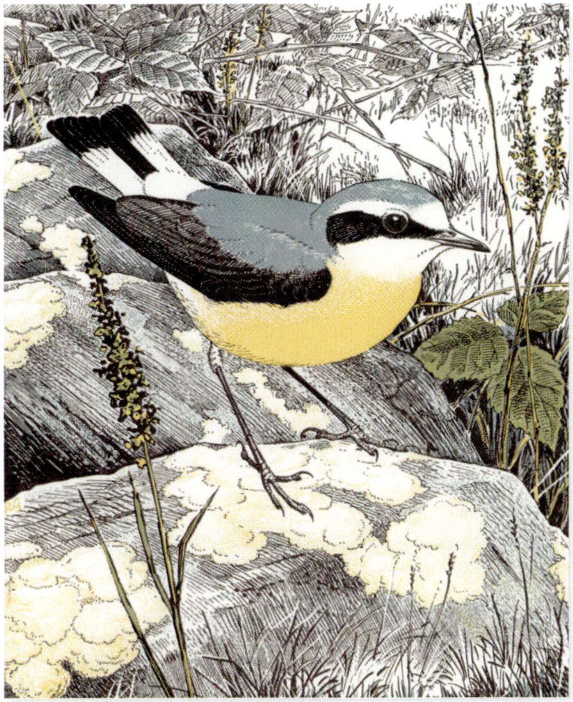

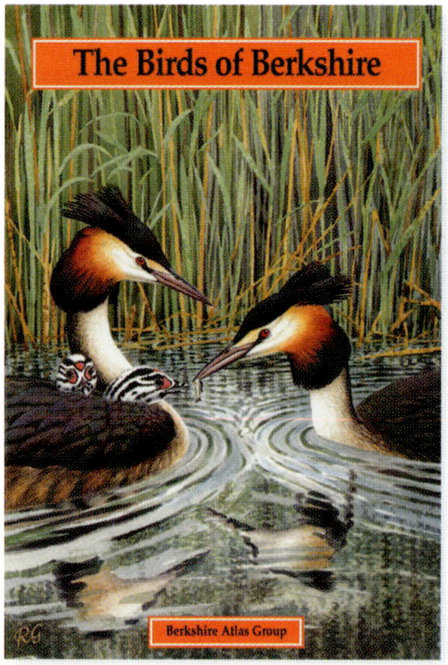

The Birds of Berkshire (The Berkshire Atlas Group, 1996)

In 2003 the Club changed its name from Reading Ornithological Club to Berkshire Ornithological Club, a move that had been under consideration for quite some time. It makes much more sense to cover the county rather than the original area of five miles around Reading. In those early days there were far fewer cars and membership was largely confined to people living in the town's immediate locality. Practically every county now, of whatever size, has its own ornithological grouping and proudly publishes reports, avifaunas and atlases covering its area. Berkshire is no different and in the late eighties a committee consisting of the Berkshire Atlas Group and others met together to produce its own book: *The Birds of Berkshire* published by The Berkshire Atlas Group, Reading, in 1996. I was invited to join as Art Editor and rounded up a team of bird artists to illustrate every species recorded in the county. For the jacket I painted a family of Great Crested Grebes, one of the birds I had been so involved with in the Club's (and my) earliest days. Now a working party is far advanced in producing a second edition of *The Birds of Berkshire* which will be an absolutely up-to-date picture of the county's avifauna, along with the results of the second local atlas. This involved members throughout Berkshire visiting every tetrad (a square of 2 km × 2 km based on the National Grid kilometre squares familiar to users of Ordnance Survey maps) to record, in as much detail as possible, the status of its birdlife. New illustrations of all species have been drawn and I have designed a jacket featuring that other special bird, both for me and the county – the Little Ringed Plover. This time I have cut a full-colour linocut print which, in part, will be a personal tribute to the late Ken Simmons who had given me so much early encouragement.

Looking back over the last sixty-four years I can see how much the involvement with my own home town Club has meant, and how indebted I am for all that it has given me. There are many other aspects quite apart from those covered in this book. The Club played an important

Illustration for the jacket of the second edition of *The Birds of Berkshire.* Little Ringed Plover, linocut

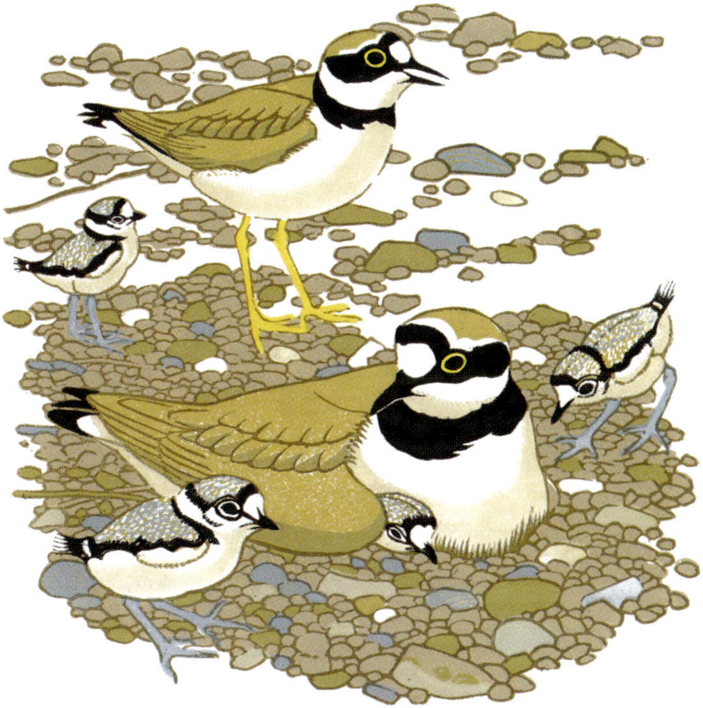

part in the 1960 'Exhibition by Contemporary Bird Painters', held in the Reading Museum and Art Gallery, which led directly to the formation of the Society of Wildlife Artists in 1964. The Society, which will hold its 50th Annual Exhibition in October 2013, has become established as the leading wildlife art body in Europe. The personal friendships and co-operation with many members of the Club has been of inestimable value, particularly with the Recorders responsible for the Annual Reports which I was allowed to embellish. From the start the officers tolerated and encouraged a small boy with lots of enthusiasm and some skill, and helped him along. I am eternally grateful and hope that I have managed to make some return in gratitude for the opportunities given to me.

Two Rivers Press has been publishing in and about Reading since 1994. Founded by the artist Peter Hay (1951–2003), the press continues to delight readers, local and further afield, with its varied list of individually designed, thought-provoking books.

Berkshire Ornithological Club (formerly Reading Ornithological Club) was founded in 1947 to promote education about and study of wild birds, their habitats and conservation in the Berkshire area. Membership is open to anyone interested in birds and bird-watching, beginner or expert, local patch enthusiast or international twitcher. The Club organises a full programme of events with indoor evening meetings and outdoor field meetings. It publishes a regular Newsletter and a Berkshire Bird Report.